Dedicated to Patsy,
Ellie (the best selling author of the future),
Charlotte & Shannon
And with thanks to
Hayley
for all her on-going help and patience.

Contents

Conclusion

Introduction

This book should probably be entitled **How to pay off your mortgage as quickly as possible!** As that is what it is really intended to illustrate. I hope it will focus on and explain the genuine desires, ambitions and long-term goals of so many people to have their mortgage cleared, **at the earliest point they can reasonably achieve.**

Mortgages are generally considered to be a weight on one's shoulders as they are a debt that is encumbered (normally) on the family home and which demands people's attention on a month-by-month basis. For many the mortgage on the home is the largest financial outgoing that we pay each month and simply ensuring that we pay that mortgage each month is the driving force that gets us out of bed in the morning. Unlike other borrowing there is an added **detrimental psychological angle** to having a mortgage as a result. When considering one's finances on a day-to-day basis, generally the first bill that has to be paid – even before feeding the family – is paying the mortgage.

Many people – understandably – see it is a major life goal to own their home outright. By clearing or repaying a mortgage, and thereby being free of the monthly financial commitment that a mortgage entails, will very likely give an individual or a family far greater life choices. Such choices might include the option to consider moving home, possibly downsizing and releasing equity to assist with retiring early, helping the children get on the housing ladder themselves or providing the financial freedom to set up a business. When there is the burden of a mortgage lender's charge hanging over the home, even if there is no real risk the lender will ever take possession, there is always an element of doubt that, potentially, if things do go wrong in life you could end up losing your home, even if this is fairly unlikely in reality.

I have spent a great deal of my time in my professional capacity trying to help people understand the importance of prioritising their financial matters and I fully appreciate that there are vast demands on one's finances on a day-to-day basis. However, there are some absolute basics that you should seek to achieve over time. Apart from the day-to-day demands of raising your family, you should also give some thought and put plans in place for:

- Ensuring that your loved ones are protected in the event of your or your partner's death or serious illness;
- Investing money for the future;
- Planning your retirement;
- Caring for elderly relatives;

Clearing or repaying the mortgage – always a primary consideration when thinking about the stability of one's long-term financial security.

Money is never important in its own right: it is the consequences of what you do with money that is of most significance. It is how it allows you to support your family, to enjoy life, to travel, to be healthy – to make good choices for yourself and those around you – that will help you make a good life for yourself.

4

There are arguments, which I will touch upon later in this book, that you should never pay off a mortgage or should defer repaying for as long as possible. There is an argument that states that the interest cost of borrowing against a house is *currently* so inexpensive that you may be better off using the money for other purposes – this is the so-called 'leverage argument'.

There are many instances where this has validity. There are no rules that state doing this or that in every case is always the right thing to do. I have met many people over the years that have needed to have substantial borrowing in their business that in itself provides stability for their families, provides employment opportunities, and allows the investment of time in their community.

However, from a residential home owners' perspective I think the desire to experience the feeling of having complete ownership of one's own home is a very powerful factor indeed and it is on this area that this book concentrates.

Setting the early repayment of your mortgage as a life goal and then working towards this life goal can lead to many spin-off benefits, both personal and financial – again I will cover this in detail later in these pages.

The ways of repaying your mortgage are hugely varied. This means you have many options, some of which may well be combined together. The methodology you pursue may also change as you progress over the years.

I have enjoyed helping individuals, couples and families work on these life goals and then guide them, step by step, over the years to the successful accomplishment of these goals, and all this entails for their futures.

Explaining how to clear a mortgage early is one of the areas in which I have built up expertise over the years and why I am seeking to put these thoughts, principles and basic rules together in one book. It is my hope you will pick this book up occasionally, gain some insight, and then begin the process of unencumbering your own home. I have seen on many occasions the immense satisfaction and pleasure that clearing a mortgage can provide as this furnishes greater life choices and benefits in other areas of life.

I hope you find the ideas and thoughts in the following pages of use. With very best wishes:

Darren Fisher
Author

Chapter 1 - Why should you pay off your mortgage early?

"Start with the end in mind. "
— **Stephen R. Covey, 'The 7 Habits of Highly Effective People'**

Much written about money and a great deal of the emphasis when it comes to personal financial planning tends to be about the subject of money itself! This statement, however contradictory it may sound, has firm foundations.

The fact is money itself means absolutely nothing on its own merits. If you think of your life and all that is important to you then, at best, money is a means to an end.

The things that are truly important tend to be the happiness and health of you and your family, or perhaps memories made from family holidays through to something as small and relatively insignificant as the smell of a wild flower, the beautiful view across an ocean from a cliff top, and so on.

The pursuit of a fortune or the accumulation of wealth has no meaning unless it is attached to something bigger and more – much more – meaningful.

However, the argument around this does not end there. There is considerable evidence that behavioural factors in finance are far more important to genuinely good financial outcomes than is generally realised.

This is a subject with a bit of depth and we do not need to cover it here. Suffice it to say, it is **how you think about your finances** that makes a big difference to how successful your long-term financial planning might be.

If we combine these two points together – finances being the means to an end rather than being the end in their own right, and how you should think about your finances in a positive and constructive way – then we can start to see why paying off a mortgage is a highly prized goal.

The financial argument in paying off a mortgage early is certainly a real one, but it is not just a purely financial one. The peace of mind and sense of accomplishment that you will feel once you have unencumbered your home, your family and your finances cannot be underestimated.

In so many respects it is the non-financial factors that hold far greater sway and which have the greater meaning, as is so often the case in these matters.

I am suggesting that the simple positive act of thinking creatively about this subject and setting out to pay off your mortgage early will **create its own positive spin-off benefits.**

If you were to adopt my favoured method of organising your finances, then you would begin to plan to a great extent around short-, medium- and long-term financial goal setting – let's call this **building a financial plan for the Future**.

The common goal of aiming to pay off your mortgage **early** forces the homeowner to make a number of short- as well as long-term assumptions, which include looking at how exactly these goals can be achieved.

Stephen Covey in his book 'The Seven Habits of Highly Effective People' states that when starting a substantial project, such as paying off a mortgage that you should always 'start with the end in mind'. Paying off a mortgage early can be a huge undertaking that can be quite daunting but focussing and narrowing in on that successful 'final goal' is actually the correct starting point.

Deciding the eventual 'final goal' in advance begins a 'thought process', which in itself creates a 'planning process'. That 'thought process' moves the goal to a series of 'what if?' questions and a modelling of one's finances both now and well into the future.

The modelling starts to look at the outcomes from the 'what if?' questions mapped out over many years.

- **What if I save more today?** Where can I make cost savings in my day-to-day finances so that I can afford to save more? Could I do without that daily latte in order to save that extra money that I need to help me make an extra payment each month on my mortgage?
- **What if I double the amount I am saving?** Where else can savings be made? Lowering home insurance and utility costs? Vehicle costs? Eating out at cheaper restaurants? One less holiday a year? etc.
- **What if want to retire five, ten or even fifteen years early?** How do I get my mortgage cleared in good time in order to be able to retire earlier than planned? Most people who have already retired would agree that in order to have financial and personal peace of mind that it is almost essential that any debt including any mortgage are repaid prior to actually retiring.
- **What if I pay myself more from my business or give myself a pay rise?** If I'm running a business is it feasible for me to increase my income by taking annual one-off dividends or if

I'm employed can I earn commissions or bonuses which will allow me to partially pay down my mortgage?

- **What if I can reduce my tax payable each year?** Am I managing my affairs as tax efficiently as possible so that I am making the best use of all the income that I have available to me?
- **Am I prepared to get myself a second part-time job if it allows me to earn extra money that could be used to pay down my mortgage more quickly?** This of course depends on your home and family situation but could be a worthwhile consideration.
- **When that home improvement loan finishes in two years' time or those school fees come to an end can I then plough those monthly savings into my mortgage each month?**

Bear in mind at this stage of the exercise we are essentially asking ourselves thought-provoking questions only. Writing down a list of cost savings and getting these cost savings into a list or spread sheet format will help solidify these thoughts. You can then effectively change and amend these thoughts and assumptions over time.

By making various assumptions about your future finances you can also start to see how the pattern changes in the future. You will be shedding light on what is important, what is feasible and where your own priorities lie.

If you walk into the office of a skilled financial planner and ask for advice on how you can pay off your mortgage early because you have set this as one of your key life goals, your financial planner will start a process with you which is very similar to that described above. Once discussed and agreed this will give you huge benefits in many ways.

Financial planners use tools called 'cash flow modelling calculators' that produce a forward-thinking example of how your finances could look in the future based on certain assumptions. We use examples of cash flow modelling later in this book when we illustrate the benefits of overpaying a mortgage and the savings that can be made over time.

We will also consider the implication that, in order to achieve the goal of repaying your mortgage early, you should impose some serious discipline onto your finances and on-going thinking. A desire to save relentlessly will – without doubt – make you more successful in achieving your objectives in clearing your mortgage early but will also have knock-on benefits for the rest of your financial planning.

When I meet people who have this desire to clear their mortgage early, I also see that they are generally highly motivated in every other area of their financial planning.

I would strongly advise that if you do not have this objective in place at the moment, put it in place now. Begin the thought processes that will carry you towards this final goal - by applying the steps that we outline in this book – and do it without delay. It will enrich you in many ways.

Chapter 2 - Formulating a Plan of Action

A wise man was once asked: 'How do you eat an elephant?' After a little thought he replied: 'One bite at a time.' The same applies to paying off a mortgage early. Unless you are very fortunate and are able to earn, inherit or receive enough money to clear your mortgage outright, it is likely that you are going to have to set a plan of action to repay your mortgage 'one bite at a time'.

If you have read this far into the book then I presume you have a clear and specific agenda and are pretty serious about learning how to pay down your mortgage as quickly as possible.

However, in my experience, plainly stating 'I want to pay off my mortgage as soon as possible' is simply not enough. You need to have a plan that is written down, that is achievable and that is reviewed on a very regular basis.

Let's take a look at some proven steps in formulating a plan of action or a simple goal-setting exercise that will help you achieve what could be a very large undertaking:

1. **You must have a specific and sharply defined long-term objective.**
2. **You must then have smaller manageable 'bite-size chunks' that lead you to the eventual long-term objective mentioned above.**
3. **You must write down this plan and place it in an easily visible place.**
4. **You must regularly revisit the written plan to ensure that you are on track to achieving this long-term goal.**

5. **You must think about this plan at least once every day.**

6. **You must continually rewrite and revisit these plans with a view to achieving your final goal.**

So taking each of the six points mentioned above:

1. You must have a specific and sharply defined long-term aim.

Your long-term goal needs to be very clear. In order for you to achieve your other goals – whether these be retiring early, helping your children get on the housing ladder or perhaps starting a business, it is likely that losing the burden of paying a mortgage each month is likely to open up your options considerably. Ask yourself the question: 'If I want to retire early, can I do so while still paying a mortgage?' The answer to that question will probably be 'no' so there you have your first long-term goal. Be very clear in your long-term objective because everything else that you work towards will finish at this end point.

2. You must then have smaller manageable 'bite-size goals' which lead you to the eventual long-term objective mentioned above

Now these short-term goals could be as simple as: 'We will definitely pay an extra £300 per month off our mortgage this year.' Or perhaps: 'At the end of the year I will use my annual bonus to repay £15,000 off the mortgage.' Or: 'Within five years our mortgage balance will not be higher than £100,000 and we will ensure that we have made occasional lump sum and regular monthly overpayments in order to achieve this.'

The important point here is that you must TAKE ACTION and make yourself ACCOUNTABLE for those actions. You must actually do what you have said that you will do – arrange that monthly overpayment, make that lump sum payment, take the proceeds from that pay out and make those extra payments.

Once you have come to the end of the first short-term goal you then need to review your situation. Look at where you stand financially and then MAKE ANOTHER short-term goal, and another, and another, working through each short-term goal each month or each year until you have achieved your long-term objective.

You need to be responsible for your goals, be demanding and be respectful of your own situation and for the need to achieve what needs to be achieved in the long term.

KEEP FOCUSED, WRITE IT DOWN and KEEP REVISITING your goals.

3.   **You must write down this plan and place it where it is easily visible**

It doesn't matter where you put the plan, whether it is on your fridge, in the study or on your phone. The act of writing something down and regularly seeing its written goals creates a need for accountability. It creates a need to continually satisfy that long-term objective and will ensure that the goal that is set is kept at the forefront of your mind and WILL BE achieved on an on-going basis.

4. **You must regularly revisit the written plan to ensure that you are on track to achieving this long-term aim**

Make a routine of sitting down and looking at the goals that have been set and ensure that they are on track. If not on track, accept accountability and do something about it – either take action or revisit those goals. If you are ahead of the game then give yourself a pat on the back – if you are behind, either rework the written goals or figure out how you can get yourself ahead again.

5. **You must think about these goals at least once every day**

Create a habit:

> *At the end of the day we are accountable to ourselves – our success is a result of what we do.* (Catherine Pulsifer)

To form a habit you must visualise the day that you pay off your mortgage and how this will impact your life. Look at your goals daily, in whatever form suits you, but make sure you do it every day. There is nothing wrong with dreaming.

6. **You must continually rewrite and revisit these plans with a view to achieving your final goal**

Once you have managed to achieve a goal, however small, then sit down and rewrite the next stage of the goal. If you have managed to reduce your mortgage from £200,000 to £180,000 using a series of overpayments and lump sum payments, how do you take it to the next stage that might be, say, reducing it to £150,000? Write it down, think about it, visualise it and plan for the next stage. Follow the steps above and you will be quickly on the road to reducing your mortgage debt.

Chapter 3 - The financial argument – paying off a mortgage as quickly as possible

Most of us inherently understand the power of compounding when it comes to money and in particular saving and investing.

Before looking at how compounding works in reverse when it comes to borrowing let's begin by looking at some simple examples of why compounding is so powerful.

There's a famous legend about the origin of chess that goes like this. When the inventor of the game showed it to the emperor of India, the emperor was so impressed by the new game that he said to the man: 'Name your reward!' The man responded:

> *Oh emperor, my wishes are simple. I only wish for this. Give me one grain of rice for the first square of the chessboard, two grains for the next square, four for the next, eight for the next and so on for all 64 squares, with each square having double the number of grains as the square before.*

The emperor agreed, amazed that the man had asked for such a small reward – or so he thought. After a week, his treasurer came back and informed him that the reward would add up to an astronomical sum, far greater than all the rice that **could conceivably be produced in many centuries!**

Here's another example. You are offered a job that lasts for seven weeks. You get to choose your salary.

Either you get £100 for the first day, £200 for the second day, £300 for the third day, and so on. Each day you are paid £100 more than the day before.

Or you get 1 penny for the first day, 2 pence for the second day, and 4 pence for the third day. Each day you are paid double what you were paid the day before.

If you choose option one, well done, you will be wealthy. You will have earned £122,500 – great pay indeed for seven weeks of work.

However, if you chose option two . . . You will quite easily become the richest person in the world and the richest who has ever lived with a total of £5,629,499,534,213.11!

Compounding at the doubling level is indeed spectacular. But even at lower levels it has power. Imagine twins, Jane and John, both inheriting £30,000 on their 21st birthday. Both decide to save the money until they retire, at age 65.

Jane saves or invests and gets a 7.0% per year rate of return after all costs and taxes. John does the same but only gets 3.5% per year. Clearly Jane will have more money at 65, but how much more?

Jane will have just over £450,000 more! The compounding effect of returns is magnified dramatically given time.

When it comes to borrowing the roles are reversed, in the sense that the 'power' comes from **eradicating** the compounding effect.

If you have borrowing costing you 10% per year then it can be shown most easily using the following examples:

Imagine you take out a loan of £20,000 over ten years at a cost of 10% per year (i.e. the interest cost or annual percentage rate – APR). That will cost you £264 per month to repay the interest and capital in ten years' time while the total borrowing cost (the total cost of the interest payments) over this period is £11,714.

However, before you take out the loan you look at your finances and decide that, actually, you can afford to pay more each month so decide to take the loan over six years and agree to pay £371 per month. You would actually reduce the interest cost of your loan down to a total of £6,677.

You have saved yourself nearly £ 7,000 in interest costs over the course of the loan!

Remember – it is ALWAYS in the banks or mortgage lender's interest for you to have longer-term loans and mortgages, as they will maximise their interest charge and profitablity over the longer term. Short-term loans, if affordable, are far more efficient and far less expensive to the borrower. Don't default to a longer term simply because the mortgage adviser writes it on the application form without first giving this some serious thought.

In the example above the compounding starts to work in reverse: the more you overpay each month, the quicker you clear your borrowing and the greater this saving will be. If you are able to take three years off a ten-year loan term it will have a greater beneficial impact on the overall cost of the borrowing than if you take just a year off the term.

It is important to note there are two parts to this cost, the actual interest rate itself – we will discuss how to reduce this later in the book – and the period that interest is being applied for.

Mortgages are a loan just like any other, with the possible exception that mortgages tend to be linked to home ownership and secured by and on the main family home.

However, mortgages are different in one way from most other loans – they are almost always long term, for example typically 25–35 years, and sometimes even longer.

This matters, because if the overall total cost of a mortgage is determined by the interest charged **and the time the interest is applied**, then you have a long period over which this occurs. If you can shorten this period you start to magnify the **cost saving** massively.

Let us now apply our examples to mortgages specifically.

We will use a **£250,000 mortgage** set up over **25 years** and assume the cost of borrowing is at a rate of **5.0% per annum**. We will also assume the mortgage is structured on a capital and interest repayment basis so that the entire loan is repaid at the end of the term. Finally in this scenario you will be asked to pay **£1,462** per month.

Assuming that interest rates do not change over that 25-year period the total amount repayable over the term of the mortgage – and therefore the total amount paid for this mortgage – will be a staggering **£438,600**. Taking off the £250,000 borrowed leaves a total interest cost over the term of the mortgage of **£188,600**.

Now let's say, having thought long and hard about your finances, that you decide to pay the mortgage off over **20 years** instead:

- Your monthly repayment will be **£1,650.00.**
- The total amount repayable over the full 20-year term will be **£396,000**; therefore the loan will cost you **£146,000** in interest costs.

Let's go one step further and look at reducing the term to **15 years**:

- Your monthly repayment will be **£1,977.00.**
- The total amount repayable over the 15 years will be **£355,860** therefore the loan will cost you **£105,860** in interest costs.

The comparison in simple tabular form is as follows:

Pay off your mortgage after	Total interest cost
25 years	**£188,600**
20 years	**£146,000**
15 years	**£105,860**

(The table assumes that interest rates have not changed over the mortgage term. E&OE)

As many people are not necessarily mathematically orientated, I would like to clarify a further point.

After looking at those figures and comparing the numbers you might say: 'Ah, but I haven't really reduced the cost that much because I have had to pay more on a monthly basis in the meantime.'

While yes, this is true more has indeed been paid out each month, but these extra payments are benefiting you rather then detrimentally costing you money each month.

That is ultimately the point of this exercise. The concept is quite simple – the quicker you can pay off the mortgage, the quicker you remove the interest that is being charged on that mortgage and the less physical time you are committed to the mortgage company each month. This adds up to the cost saving described above.

As mortgages tend to be very long-term commitments and at what can be eye watering high levels of borrowing making most other personal loans, credit cards, etc. pale into insignificance, the value to you and your family of the cost saving of repaying this mortgage debt early can be enormous.

This is why clearing a mortgage as early as possible makes perfect sense for most people. However, two points about this should be clarified. Firstly, the examples shown above are not necessarily 'reality'. The realisation of this tends not to dawn on most people until long after they have started paying their mortgage, and once used to paying a mortgage payment over, say, a 25-year period will, because of the increased cost, struggle to switch with ease to a 15-year repayment cycle.

Secondly, I also have to acknowledge and consider the counter-argument: why you should consider **not** paying off your mortgage.

I will deal with this in the next chapter.

Chapter 4 - The argument for NOT paying off your mortgage

The financial argument for clearing your mortgage that was dealt with in the previous chapter does have some basic flaws. Before we move on to the practicalities and actual solutions to clearing a loan early let us also consider the other side of the argument.

Remember, at this stage, we are dealing with financial aspects only. I will maintain throughout the pages of this book that the personal and emotional 'non-financial aspects' remain highly important. Psychologically, clearing a mortgage is a wonderful life goal to achieve.

However, if we stick solely to the financial arguments let us look at the so-called flaws in the concept outlined in the last chapter.

There are essentially three and they all relate to the same sort of point:

1. To voluntarily overpay your mortgage each month you will have to allocate extra money each and every month to pay down your debt, money you will almost certainly not be contractually required to pay by the mortgage lender (unless you have committed to this). The same applies to occasional lump sums that you may choose to make. So, you are choosing to allocate additional money now towards the mortgage as opposed to spending it on the family, the house, having holidays or saving/investing elsewhere.

2. In recent years, the interest cost of a residential mortgage has tended to be far less expensive than other forms of borrowing, possibly so much so that you may be able to invest in other

assets and potentially get a higher rate of return on the money than the value of the interest being charged on the mortgage itself.

3.   The property boom has been so well-established in the UK over the last fifty years or so that there is a school of thought that you should maximise property borrowing wherever possible and get as much leverage on the (supposedly!) ever increasing property market. The point here is that you can potentially do more with your money – or make better use of it – if you use it in some other way rather than clearing your mortgage debt.

These are extremely subjective matters and I believe in most cases they can be shown to be very weak counter-arguments.

I will deal with each one at a time and then summarise across all three.

Argument no. 1

To voluntarily overpay your mortgage each month you will have to allocate extra money each and every month to pay down your debt, money you will almost certainly not be contractually required to pay by the mortgage lender (unless you have committed to this). The same applies to occasional lump sums that you may choose to make. So, you are choosing to allocate additional money now towards the mortgage as opposed to spending it on the family, the house, having holidays or saving/investing elsewhere.

There is no doubt, as none of us have a crystal ball, that the idea of allocating your time and hard-earned money on saving as opposed to spending is a reasonable challenge. 'Live for the day' is a maxim many would subscribe to. Who knows how long you will live? What challenges will tomorrow or next year bring?

This is a classic position which, if followed logically, would mean you would never plan long term. The statistics are quite clear: most people – a huge proportion – live well into retirement. There is an even bigger problem if you 'live for today' and then suddenly find that tomorrow arrives and you haven't made any provision for it.

Possibly the most important financial discipline anyone can have is to save for the future. This involves salting money away on a regular basis. The net effect of reducing a mortgage quickly is to clear the cost of a mortgage, which is in effect creating a risk-free return.

The overpayment is **not** additional spending – it is, at the end of the day, a form of saving.

Now, if it disrupts your short-term plans and stops you from having holidays or sending your children to nursery or some other form of immediate gain, then the balance between your savings and spending may need reviewing. However, if you can find a way to balance this out, which could involve wider planning moves, then you will get the 'knock-on' advantage I mentioned earlier: that side effect – the financial impact gain of simply choosing to accelerate a mortgage repayment.

Forcing yourself to do this can often create further funds later (as a result of your wider financial planning steps). This means you can rebalance and get the mortgage repayment accelerated AND still have exactly what you need for today.

I cannot emphasise enough the psychological factors here, which so often turn out to provide positive financial advantages.

Argument no. 2

In recent years, the interest cost of a residential mortgage has tended to be far less expensive than other forms of borrowing, possibly so much so that you may be able to invest in other assets and potentially get a higher rate of return on the money than the value of the interest being charged on the mortgage itself.

If this argument really makes sense then why wouldn't you borrow every last penny you could secure against your property and invest any balance in other assets such as rental property or stocks and shares?

For example, if you have a £350,000 property and a £200,000 mortgage, surely you should borrow or re-mortgage as much as the market allows, say £300,000, and then take that extra £100,000 and invest it?

Most people would agree that this is NOT a good idea at all, and most professional advisers would be sanctioned if they suggested this as a matter of course. Therefore, generally speaking, this is not a suitable course of action, the reason primarily being that there is no guarantee that interest rates will remain as low as they have been in the last few years. Interest rates dropped to an all-time low in 2009 because of the extreme recession that had started in 2008. To protect the economy the government pumped vast amounts of money into the financial system which included dropping bank base rates from 5.75% in July 2007 to 0.50% in March 2009. Interest rates then remained at an all-time low for nearly ten years until they began to rise again in late 2017 and early 2018.

The interest rate decreases in 2008/9 were dramatic because of the severity of the recession at the time. Since then, and up to the time of writing, interest rates in the UK – and indeed across the world – have begun to rise again, albeit gently.

I still have bitter memories of paying my first mortgage in the late 1980's at an eye-watering mortgage interest rate of 15.40%, which at the time was the norm. Mortgage interest rates were far higher then and consequently the percentage of household income needed to fund basic housing costs was dramatically higher than it is now.

We all hope (most sincerely) that mortgage rates do not increase to the levels of the late 1980's and early 1990's but this is always a possibility. While rates have begun to rise there is now an entire generation which has not known anything other than very low interest rates.

The second reason why this is not a good idea is that investing in other assets such as rental or commercial property or a stocks and shares portfolio carries no guarantee of positive investment returns. Investing can be a complex and expensive business and should only be considered when taking professional financial advice.

Overall, having a mortgage because it is 'a good investment' makes limited financial sense and doesn't present a compelling reason to ignore options to accelerate repayment.

Argument no. 3

The property boom has been so well-established in the UK over the last fifty years or so that there is a school of thought that you should maximise property borrowing wherever possible and get as much leverage* on the (supposedly!) ever increasing property market.

This is the most dangerous argument of all, the so-called 'you can't go wrong with bricks and mortar' concept.

It is a constant amazement to me that when property is discussed in the media there can be a complete lack of basic questioning around how it is economically sustainable for an asset such as residential property to defy the laws of economic gravity.

Just like any other asset, property sales are driven by supply and demand. Very simplistically, when there is great demand, house prices will rise and when demand is low house prices will falter. Remember for every seller there has to be a buyer.

And then, why is property seen as something which the more expensive it gets, the better it is for the economy and society – as if this makes people richer across all of society?

** **Leverage** is an investment strategy of using borrowed money — specifically borrowed capital — to increase the potential return of an investment.*

In my experience when **any** asset starts to be considered almost risk free we are close to the day when a nasty shock will come. I am not predicting future property prices, but I am stating that the risks, from a financial point of view, have historically been wildly underestimated. The chances of a big fall and/or a long period of sustained value reduction in respect of UK property is much higher than many seem to appreciate.

This being the case, the more one is leveraged on an asset that is falling in value the more dangerous (and stressful) it is. Or to put it the other way round – having less leverage is better, so clearing a mortgage down as quickly as possible is better than not clearing it down at all.

If property continues to rise in value the homeowner still benefits from that increase in local property prices, both psychologically as well as financially.

Overall I believe the view of property held by most people today, spurred on by UK governments which have made home ownership a holy grail, has led to a breakdown in the fundamental laws of good financial practice and economic competence.

While there is rarely a right thing to do in every case or circumstance, in the main clearing debt is going to benefit people and represents a sound financial discipline. Likewise, clearing debt more quickly is going to produce better financial outcomes than doing so slowly or more modestly.

The arguments for not clearing a mortgage may stand up in some cases, but not as a general practice and those cases will be in the minority.

Chapter 5 - Understanding good debt and bad debt – pay off the bad debt first!

It is fairly reasonable to ask the question 'How can any debt be good debt?' but there are some forms of debt that provide a positive outcome for you in the long run. Let's look at some examples of 'good debt':

1. A **mortgage** on a house or business premises would be considered 'good debt'. This is because you are using a mortgage to purchase an asset, which hopefully will appreciate in value over time. Mortgage debt tends to be fairly inexpensive from an interest rate perspective and you will have a structured repayment plan – often between 10 and 30 years.

2. **Student debt** would also be classed as 'good debt'. Obtaining a university degree in the UK is far from inexpensive, but if it leads you to a well paid and productive career then this has to be a price that is well worth paying. I do not intend to go into the politics and detail of student debt in this book but a newly qualified doctor who has spent many years at university learning their trade will add great value to their community and eventually their own increased earnings will mean that they can over time afford to clear this student debt.

3. **Investing in a business** should also be considered 'good debt'. Anything that drives a career or provides employment opportunities for you, your family and other members of your community has to be thought of as an investment rather than a cost. I am sure that there cannot be a successful business in the

UK that has not had to borrow at some point or other – whether for premises, stock, equipment or staff.

On the other hand, bad debt is any form of debt that drains your finances rather than helping you grow your wealth. Bad debt tends to be expensive and inflexible and offers poor value for money. Examples of bad debt would be:

1. **Credit cards** – particularly those with very high levels of interest that are poorly managed. Credit card providers will often offer introductory terms which make it appear that using credit cards on a day-to-day basis is attractive but they do this to lull customers into a false sense of security. Before you know it the introductory offer is over and the credit card provider is charging you exorbitant amounts of interest on any outstanding debt that is left on the card.

2. **Store cards.** As with credit cards, store cards will offer new customers initial discounts or incentives in order to attract them with a view to hitting them with high levels of interest at a later date.

3. **Bank overdrafts.** Used wisely bank overdrafts can help individuals and businesses with their cash flow but they do need to be used properly and within the limits that have been agreed with the bank. Any overdraft that exceeds its agreed limit will be expensive to run and will create chaos with one's finances.

4. **Pay-day lenders.** These are quite simply the most expensive form of short-term credit. Pay-day lenders offer immediate,

short-term loans at often exceedingly high levels of interest with little or no security. In the context of this book they are simply to be avoided wherever possible.

Before you start thinking about clearing your mortgage it generally makes financial sense to clear any more expensive outstanding debts first. By doing this you will reduce the level of interest that you pay, release further net spendable household income and get a good handle on your finances. Perhaps draw up a list or spreadsheet that details the level of personal debt that you have, the interest being charged and any level of early payment penalty that may apply. The general rule is to concentrate on repaying the most expensive debt first.

If you have credit card debt consider being a 'rate tart' and move the outstanding balances from provider to provider who are offering more competitive short-term rates while you are paying down the debt. At the time of writing this book there were plenty of short term 0% interest rate credit cards available (albeit there is a fee to obtain these cards) but there are other competitive long-term rates available (again probably a fee will apply). Manage your debts properly, understand what you have and put together a payment plan to clear the most expensive unsecured debts first. This way you will have further disposable income to clear your mortgage and also improve your general standard of living.

Chapter 6 - Ensure you have sufficient emergency cash savings behind you

Good old-fashioned budgeting logic says it's always worthwhile having some emergency cash savings in place to cover any one-off emergencies that may occur. This is true of course unless you have expensive short-term debt (credit cards, store cards, etc.) that needs to be cleared as quickly as possible. In contrast, for those who are 'bad-debt free', having an emergency cash fund is also a very good idea indeed.

Emergencies come in all shapes and sizes – whether it be urgent car repairs, the boiler breaking down or helping family members. In my house, there are always things that need to be paid for!

Even more important is to have some form of cash savings behind you when drastic and unexpected changes to, say, employment occur such as redundancy or you have a sudden unexpected downturn in your business.

Budgeting properly for such emergencies and ensuring that you have a readily available cash sum will give you the reassurance that you have money set aside to deal with any urgent problems.

It's always a good idea to keep an emergency fund in a cash savings account – three to six months' worth of cash is a good guide, enough to live on if you lost your job, for example. If you have additional income because of, say, a pay rise and you are thinking of overpaying your mortgage, then ensure that you build up an emergency cash fund first.

This applies even if the calculator shows you'd be better off overpaying your mortgage. It's what's known as 'a premium for liquidity'. In other words, it's sacrificing some interest for easy access to cash when needed.

Remember that short-term borrowing is generally very expensive. It will be completely self-defeating to commit to overpaying your mortgage but then have to borrow using credit cards because you have not managed your short-term finances properly.

Chapter 7 – Back to basics – the different types of mortgage

Now would probably be a good time to revisit some basics relating to the most common form of mortgages available in the UK. I will oversimplify a little when explaining some features about mortgages themselves, but this is simply for the purpose of retaining a focus upon the bigger picture, which is all about learning how to pay off your mortgage as quickly as possible.

So, put simply, there are two overarching forms of mortgage repayment. You can organise your mortgage either on a **capital and interest repayment** basis or on an **interest only** basis. The difference is very important, especially with regard to the bigger picture we are considering here.

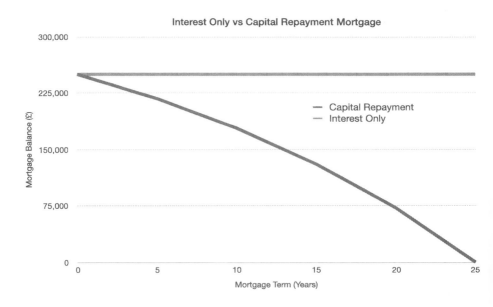

With a capital and interest repayment mortgage, you are entering into a borrowing situation whereby you are going to pay the mortgage company, the lender, a monthly payment which comprises both an element of interest and an element of capital repayment. The lender will calculate the amount of interest and capital repayable monthly so you repay the mortgage precisely at the end of the term.

For example, if you borrow £250,000 over 25 years at an interest rate of 5.0% per year you will pay a total monthly repayment of £1,461.

Pay that every month for 25 years and, assuming that those payments are maintained throughout, at the end of that term you will be guaranteed to have cleared your mortgage.

That, of course, assumes that the interest rate being charged on the mortgage always remains at 5.0% per year. If interest rates go up your monthly payment will increase; correspondingly, if they go down your monthly payment will decrease.

With a capital and interest repayment mortgage you know if you pay the exact amount required by the lender each and every month, you will finally reduce your mortgage balance to zero.

There is a little understood but exceedingly important point you need to be aware of with a capital and interest repayment mortgage and that is that your outstanding capital amount is not being paid off 'evenly'.

You should be aware and understand that in all cases the rule of thumb for any mortgage is that the lender makes its money 'first and foremost'. Let's look at some examples.

Let's assume that you maintain your £250,000 mortgage for the first five years of the 25-year term. In simple terms you might reasonably have expected to have paid off a fifth of your loan (because five years is a fifth of 25 years), therefore it is also reasonable to assume that you have paid off £50,000 leaving an overall mortgage balance of around £200,000.

However, this is not the case! The actual mortgage balance will be in the region of £221,463 after five years.

Here are the outstanding balances at other key stages of the mortgage:

After 10 years	–	**£184,833**
After 15 years	–	**£137,815**
After 20 years	–	**£77,464**

The speed of repayment is slow to start with and only really picks up in the later years, increasing most dramatically towards the end of the mortgage term.

This distortion comes about as part of a 'trade off' with the mortgage lender. With a capital and interest repayment mortgage you pay an equal amount every month to help you with ensuring that your affordability is maintained and to make the mortgage payments as constant as possible throughout the whole period (ignoring, of course, interest cost fluctuations, i.e. assuming interest costs stay the same, in the example 5.0% per year).

So, when you commence your mortgage, your first payments are around £1,461 each month. The bad news is that £1,041.67 of this payment is initial interest – the rest, around £420 is used to repay a very small amount of the outstanding loan that you borrowed.

Let's look at the position after ten years. You now owe the mortgage company a mere £184,833, so in the first month of the eleventh year your interest cost is now £184,833 x 5%/12 = £770.51.

You are still paying the original £1,461 every month, so in this first month of your eleventh year, your payment is split as follows:

Mortgage interest	–	**£770.51**
Capital being repaid	–	**£690.49**

Can you see therefore that in your 121st month you are paying a capital amount off your mortgage of £690.49 whereas in your first month you were paying off only £420?

Month by month, you pay a little less interest to the mortgage company and a little more capital until you have reached the end of the term when the loan is guaranteed to be fully repaid. The most important point to realise is that, as has been mentioned previously, the mortgage lender ALWAYS makes its money first and foremost. A capital and interest repayment is distinctly loaded entirely in favour of the mortgage lender but you will have the reassurance that you are GUARANTEED to have repaid that loan at the end of the mortgage term. This is the trade-off when having a repayment mortgage.

It can be a sobering thought to suddenly realise that having been paying a mortgage for 20 years of a 25-year term you still owe 30% of that initial mortgage debt at the end of the twentieth year –

but at the end of the day that is how a repayment mortgage is structured. That is why banks and mortgage lenders offer them!

It can also be quite upsetting to realise that, having paid a repayment mortgage for ten years and then deciding to move house (as many people do), that they have paid very little off their initial mortgage and to ensure that payments are kept to an affordable level that they are then tied in to a new 25-year repayment mortgage in which the cycle starts all over again!

I will come back to some features of the capital repayment mortgage shortly, but first let us now look at the alternative – **interest only** mortgages.

An interest only mortgage is one where you enter into a loan agreement with a lender and you agree to pay them only the interest element each month. The actual repayment of the mortgage is considered and dealt with separately and left to the end of the term.

In this case you have to plan some other way of paying off the outstanding loan as you do not do so 'naturally' through the monthly payment, as you do with a repayment mortgage.

To illustrate this in practice, we will use the same example of a £250,000 mortgage with an interest rate of 5.0% per annum and a mortgage term of 25 years.

You enter into the interest only mortgage arrangement and contractually only have to pay the lender £1,041.67 in interest each month, so your monthly payment is £419.33 per month less throughout the whole of the mortgage term.

You may instantly notice a large 'problem'.

While you are paying out £419.33 less per month you are not, at any time, repaying a penny of your mortgage, whether in whole or in part at any time over the mortgage term.

Now importantly, if you have quickly done the maths, you will also have noticed that if you take this saving each month and place the £419.33 into a bank account for the whole period, it will accumulate to only £125,799 over the 25 years. That's a great deal less than the £250,000 originally borrowed.

On the surface therefore it appears that the interest only option is a very poor choice indeed, because even if you collect the amount saved each and every month you will get nowhere near the mortgage amount you originally owed and therefore will not have enough money to repay the mortgage at the end of the term.

However, this is not the true picture. To make the comparison valid you have to look harder at the £419.33 per month that you do not need to contractually pay each month – and which you can do something else with – and also look at the power of compounding returns when that money is invested elsewhere.

If this amount is invested monthly and grows at, say, 5.0% per year after costs and taxes are taken into account, then over 25 years the amount accumulated from those monthly savings plus investment growth would have grown to roughly £250,000 (the same as the initial mortgage).

Conversely, it is very important to understand that if the investment grows at, say, only 3.0% per year on the same basis (i.e. after costs and taxes) it will grow to only £187,000 approximately (which is £63,000 less than the mortgage outstanding).

However, if the investment grows at, say, 7.0% per year the sum will be around £339,000 – a significant £89,000 more than the outstanding mortgage balance.

We are seeing the power of compounding working again in this example.

Now interest only mortgages as well as capital and interest repayment mortgages have had their place over the years – but they have also had their problems. Repayment mortgages are by far the less risky option and are generally used for lower-risk domestic home mortgages, whereas 'interest only' mortgages have been used for higher risk property investment such as when buying 'buy to let' rental property.

Interest only mortgages became popular in the 1990s when mortgage finance was freely available and lenders sought to provide ever more flexible payment options. This payment flexibility, although attractive at the time because of the lower outgoings that interest only mortgages allowed, is now becoming a real problem to existing borrowers who still have those original mortgages.

The challenge is that these original borrowers could now be in a position where they now need to repay mortgage balances that are coming to the end of their mortgage terms. There are huge numbers of existing mortgage holders who are finding that they have loans that need to be repaid but who have no realistic form of mortgage repayment vehicle – because they have failed to adequately plan their mortgage repayment strategy OR those plans have been derailed due to poor investment returns or poor planning.

These existing mortgage borrowers are increasingly being forced to make a decision as to what they do with these loans when the original mortgage terms come to their end. This might now involve them refinancing to a new loan (which will likely be on a repayment basis!) or they may even be forced to sell their properties to clear the mortgage debt outright.

At the time of writing this book the UK government regulator has been having discussions with the mortgage industry to try to find acceptable ways for at least some of these borrowers to retain their interest-only mortgage loans, possibly into retirement. These 'retirement interest only mortgages' will be discussed in a later chapter.

Summary

The difference between capital repayment mortgages and interest only mortgages is that the former provide a structured monthly payment to ensure all the mortgage capital is repaid at the end of the term, whereas the latter simply requires you to pay the cost of the borrowing, i.e. the interest, with a consequently lower monthly cost. If you only pay the interest on an interest only mortgage and do not use the lower cost to instigate some form of investment plan, then you will not pay off your mortgage.

I started this chapter by saying I was oversimplifying the matter and I continue to do so. The position is rarely this simple for several reasons and this simple comparison between repayment and interest only mortgages is largely theoretical. Here are the two main reasons:

1. Laws and regulations now make interest only mortgages at best unpopular and at worst unattainable unless there is also a

formal, structured and agreed repayment or investment plan running alongside. A lender would now be deemed irresponsible if they did not ensure a customer's loan had a plan of some sort attached to ensure repayment at an appropriate future point. This may apply today but did not at many points in the past.

2. Most borrowers have far more complex financial arrangements as opposed to just having a mortgage to think about. This means the mortgage, while often a very central factor in any long-term financial planning, is just one part of a much bigger picture. Working out how to structure a mortgage, how to make the most efficient repayments, and how and when to pay the mortgage off is not going to be their only concern. For example, most people are also concerned with retirement planning, lifestyle planning and making sure their family is well catered for. The mortgage has to sit in among all of this broader financial planning and be considered in this wider context.

Chapter 8 - Fixed interest or variable interest – which is better?

The way you think about and structure your mortgage is not restricted to deciding how you repay the actual loan over the course of its term. You also need to consider at the inception of the mortgage – and very likely a few more times over the course of the remaining years – as to whether you choose to have a 'fixed rate of interest' for a set period of years or whether you will have a 'variable rate mortgage'.

Other forms of rates may be considered but for the sake of this explanation we will keep it to the following two options – **fixed** or **variable**.

A fixed rate is one where you agree with your lender that the rate of interest you pay them will be fixed at a certain level, e.g. 5.0% per year for a fixed period of time.

At the end of five years you will then (probably) move onto the standard variable rate at that time (which could be higher or lower than the variable rate today) or you could choose to move to another fixed rate if one is available. Bear in mind there is no guarantee that a new fixed rate will be offered in future years.

Fixed rates are based on a lender's expectation of long-term general interest rate movements as dictated by the market at the time. You should always remember the primary rule that mortgage lenders are commercial organisations and are therefore seeking to make a profit from you, first and foremost. They will take this into consideration when pricing fixed mortgage rates based on these long-term interest rate expectations and assumptions and if they, for example, were to offer a 5.0% fixed rate for five or ten years their expectation is that interest rates will actually be LOWER over that period. The mortgage company is therefore hoping to make a profit from their own assumptions over the course of that fixed-rate period.

However, from the customer's perspective the fixed rate will provide you with the certainty that your mortgage payments over that term will always remain the same, without the worry that if interest rates do rise your payment to the lender is going to rise. This provides considerable peace of mind over the term of the fixed rate, particularly if interest rates are likely to rise in the long term.

However, once you have agreed and accepted a fixed rate, it is set for the duration and, importantly, trying to get out of it can be exceedingly expensive.

The term offered could be anything from a very short period such as two years possibly to the entire duration of the mortgage, such as 20 years.

Variable rates are those where your interest rate charge is based on general prevailing market interest rates and could fluctuate at any time as the general rate of interest moves up or down.

Over the past few decades mortgage rates have moved from being over 10% per year to as low as 1% per year for some borrowers on special deals.

This 'swing' is huge. On a £250,000 mortgage, the variation in interest costs would be £25,000 per year to pay at a 10% interest rate and down to £2,500 per year for a 1% interest rate. That's a massive £22,500 difference!

The recent trend – at the time of writing in early 2019 – has been for interest rates to be very low and reasonably stable, with virtually no significant movement for around eight years. This, however, is unusual based on long-term historic trends.

The consideration for borrowers must always be to weigh up whether the fixed rate option, which provides certainty and a known cost for the duration of the fixed rate term, is better than the variable rate option. The variable rate could easily end up costing less, but there is no certainty and in a period of rapidly escalating market rates could also prove to be much more expensive – and even unaffordable.

When considering paying off your mortgage as quickly as possible any cost reduction in your mortgage interest is a bonus BUT you have to make a very important decision as to whether you should have a fixed or variable rate. Let's think again about our £250,000 repayment mortgage over 25 years. Simply, a 1.0% difference in interest rates makes initially a £2,500 difference a year in interest mortgage payments – that is a lot of money which potentially could be used to help fund overpayments. Consider your options carefully both initially when applying for the loan and later in the mortgage term when you may be considering moving to a new rate either by re-mortgaging or by taking a lender's existing customer loyalty rate.

Leverage

When you can think of a mortgage as a positive financial 'commodity' rather than as a negative 'financial weight around your neck' you will realise how valuable a commodity a mortgage can be. Most commonly you will use a mortgage to buy the home you live in. I accept that many people have mortgages for second properties, holiday homes or buy-to-let properties but the main mortgage is normally for your principal residence.

I have a saying that goes: 'If we didn't borrow money then we would still be living with our mothers.' In my case this is certainly true. I bought my first property at the age of 18 in 1986 with little or no money but what I did have at the time was a small deposit (provided by a family member), a salary and a good credit rating. A very nice lady in a building society saw the potential in me and agreed to allow me to leverage my very small deposit into a warm, dry and homely one-bedroomed flat. That flat was the stepping stone to the rest of my life.

There is no other investment or asset class – generally speaking – which produces the level of emotional attachment that your home does. If you buy shares in a public company or invest in government bonds, you do not also live in them, get married in them or raise your family in them. But when it comes to your home, this is what happens. It doubles up in the minds of most people as both somewhere to live but it is also considered (correctly or incorrectly) an investment.

The 'investment aspect' is a subject that I will discuss further in the next chapter – as this aspect could potentially be a dangerous one, or at least one with a certain amount of risk attached. That risk is one we may all have lost sight of in recent years.

However, the fact is that buying a property by default creates an inherent investment position which historically has worked very well, particularly for the older generation, and has historically managed to supercharge a bricks-and-mortar property into the investment of a lifetime. And quite often that is because of the 'leverage effect'.

Most ordinary people do not borrow money to invest. The plain fact is that potentially you could do so if you were in a very confident position that the investment you choose is going to rise in value quicker and higher than the cost of borrowing the money.

Of course, that would generally be considered to be very poor and even foolhardy advice, because rarely – if ever - does such a certain future return present itself.

Theoretically the position when thinking about property is relatively simple. If you can buy a property for, say, £250,000 which increased in value by an average of 7.0% per year, you are theoretically much better off doing so using borrowing, providing you can borrow at a lower rate of interest.

So if you can borrow at 5.0% per year, you could, for example, borrow £225,000 and place £25,000 of your own money down as a deposit to complete the £250,000 purchase price.

Very simply, after ten years your asset is now worth (give or take a little) £500,000 – your loan can be repaid leaving you with a 'profit' of £275,000. You have tied up or spent £25,000 of your own money plus £11,250 per year in mortgage costs for ten years. Your outlay has been £137,500 to receive a potential return of £275,000. This of course assumes that you sell the property.

Compare that to putting the £25,000 into an investment which grew at 7.0% per year, which is then worth £50,000 after ten years. You could have saved the £11,250 per year into an investment plan and if this also grew at 7.0% per year you would have the £50,000 plus the accrued savings of £155,435.

You would have a total of just over £205,000 – much less than the £275,000 in the leveraged example. This is over just ten years but because of compounding this difference would stretch ever more impressively over 20 or 25 years, which are typical mortgage terms.

Of course, the other consideration to this argument is that you also have somewhere to live while the asset is increasing in value and you are paying the mortgage each month.

Compounding and its miracle effects were discussed earlier. Now mix leverage and compounding and potentially you have lift off!

This is why many homeowners, particularly those homeowners who bought their properties many years ago and who traditionally just wanted to have a nice home to live in, have prospered so well from an investment point of view. In the normal world these people, normally safe and sensible, have become highly leveraged investors.

In this day and age, because of the risks involved financial advisers, lenders and regulators would never normally allow this type of highly leveraged position in any other form of asset class but because the property market is deemed so reliable and also because you have to live somewhere, this situation has tended to work and, certainly in the UK, has created great prosperity.

However, there is an important consideration that we have to be aware of, which we will now explore in the next chapter.

Chapter 9 - Future v. past

The leverage position works perfectly as long as the mathematics adds up in exactly the right way. More or less, for the past couple of generations, this 'leverage argument' has worked very well.

A notable exception was in the early 1990s. A number of factors coincided and property prices fell quite significantly. The Conservative government at the time had encouraged property ownership as a desirable ambition (which included offering mortgage interest rate tax relief and deep discounts on the purchase of council houses). In addition, the onset of a recession meant a steep increase in interest rates which in itself resulted in many people falling heavily into mortgage arrears. Property prices also fell significantly as supply dramatically outstripped demand and homeowners were forced into losing their homes because they simply could not afford to service the mortgages that they had taken on and mortgage lenders pursued an aggressive stance of repossessing properties where the cost of the debt that they had provided couldn't be serviced.

Negative equity exists when the value of the mortgage exceeds the value of the property. It has been quite some time since this phrase was in common use! From a personal perspective I remember interest rates on my mortgage rising to a crippling 15.40% a year and being in a position where three-quarters of my income was being used just to pay the mortgage each month. In addition, the value of our house dropped by a quarter which meant that the value of the mortgage was significantly greater than the value of the house.

Effectively we were in a very bad way. Having a family was put on hold for a few years while we fought to keep our heads above water and it was only some years later that the situation improved.

There have been other dips and periods of small decreases in the value of house prices over the years, but the general trend for the past forty years or so has been upwards. In part this can be explained by ongoing increases in earnings, which has triggered rises in demand for property which have historically pushed up prices. Remember, though, that there is no guarantee that this will continue – the next recession may be just around the corner. I have learned over the years that 'the only constant in life is change'. The mortgage market has had radical reform over recent years, resulting in it now being harder to obtain a mortgage to try to ensure that this situation doesn't happen again. However, it is important to understand that a radical shock in the economy, a change in government, a change in housing legislation or simply a lack of confidence in the housing market will have a dramatic effect on house prices.

The leverage effect works providing that property prices increase over the years due to a healthy economy and stable interest rates are maintained. It is reasonable to expect over a long period of time that this will probably continue to be the case, **but it is not a given**. There is no immutable law which states property prices must rise and this applies in the long term just as much as it does in the short.

This book is about how and why you should seek to clear a mortgage early, so the arguments about property value increases, how likely they are to continue and how much risk there is, are all fairly secondary.

However, I would like to stress that the golden rule that 'bricks and mortar' are a safe bet is one to be wary of and there is almost always more risk than one might imagine that the future may not mirror the past. The important point is to acknowledge this risk. It is a real one.

Let us therefore imagine a scenario where property prices fall over a sustained period and explore how this impacts the leverage.

Using the same example as in the previous chapter, you buy for £250,000 and use a £25,000 deposit with a £225,000 mortgage at 5.0% per year interest.

But this time over ten years property prices fall 40%, your £250,000 house is now worth £150,000. Your mortgage is either still £225,000 with an interest only mortgage or about £185,000 with a capital repayment mortgage. In both cases you are now substantially down, your £25,000 deposit plus the capital costs of repaying the loan have resulted in an overall capital loss.

You have, however, had the pleasure of living ten years in your own home. This is an important factor that I stressed in earlier chapters.

If we remove the utility of living somewhere and now focus purely on the investment side, the leverage is working against you.

No one should make plans around their property ownership based on an upward only property market scenario – that would be financially irresponsible!

Chapter 10 - Understanding the terms and conditions of your mortgage – including redemption penalties

However you choose to try and pay down your mortgage early there are a couple of points that you do need to understand before you start down this road. Put simply, it is important that you have a good grasp of the terms and conditions of your mortgage and what the mortgage lender will and what they will not allow you to do when it comes to paying down your mortgage early.

Many schemes, particularly fixed rate or initial discounted variable rates schemes that provide early year discounts, will carry redemption penalties. When taking a mortgage you effectively enter into a contract with the mortgage company, where they agree to offer you a fixed rate or a discount off their normal variable rate for a certain period of time but in order for them to make a profit from you they need you to hold the mortgage for a certain length of time. This will generally be at least the term of the fixed or discounted rate. If you keep the mortgage for the initial term then everyone is happy – you get a good rate and the mortgage lender is eventually able to make a profit from lending you that money.

Should you decide to come out of that mortgage deal, say by completely paying off the loan within the redemption period or paying a large amount off the mortgage within the redemption period, the mortgage company will levy a penalty on you, known as a 'redemption penalty'. This redemption penalty is effectively the profit margin that the mortgage company would have made from you if you had maintained the mortgage for the full term of the discounted or fixed rate period.

However . . . there is some good news: most mortgage lenders – and I say most mortgage lenders with the caveat 'some more lenders' – will allow you to make annual lump sum or overpayment amounts of say, 5.0% or up to 10.0% of the outstanding loan each year thereby giving you the flexibility of being in a position where you can, if you choose to and can afford to, pay down the mortgage by making an additional payment at any time over the remaining term of the loan.

It is essential therefore that you read and understand the mortgage offer that is provided to you at the inception of the mortgage. This details the terms and conditions of the loan including the fees that they will charge you, the terms of the rate that you have agreed to and the redemption terms should you redeem your mortgage at any time during the mortgage term.

A typical £240,000 mortgage offer will detail its terms and conditions regarding redemption penalties and overpayments in the following way:

What happens if you do not want this mortgage anymore?

Until 31ˢᵗ December 2023, an early repayment charge is payable if you repay the mortgage or vary its terms, for example by switching to another product. The early repayment charge is 5.0% of the balance outstanding at the beginning of the month in which the mortgage is repaid. The maximum charge you would pay is £12,000, plus an administration fee which is currently £145.00

After the 31st December 2023, the early repayment charge no longer applies but the administration fee, currently £145.00 is payable, if you repay the mortgage at any time.

What happens if you want to make overpayments?

An overpayment is a payment that is in addition to the minimum payment that you make each month.

You can make lump sum or regular overpayments of up £24,000, i.e. 10% of the mortgage, in each complete 12 month period from the date the mortgage starts until 31st December 2023 without having to pay an early repayment charge. Amounts above this are subject to an early repayment charge (as detailed above).

After 31st December 2023 there are no restrictions on the amount that you can overpay.

If you make an overpayment the amount you owe us will be reduced immediately, and the amount of interest you pay, will be reduced from the first day of the following month.

So looking at these terms, it is quite obvious that the mortgage company is stating very clearly what you can and what you cannot do. They are not hiding anything and are very clear in their language as well.

The first paragraph states that should you completely repay the mortgage that they will seek to charge you their 'profit margin (as discussed above)' in the form of a redemption penalty. This redemption penalty, shown in both percentage and monetary terms, is very clear and concise. Once the fixed-term period is over, i.e. on

1st January 2024, the redemption penalty will cease and the mortgage company will only charge a fixed administration fee to repay the loan.

However, the lender is prepared to allow you to repay up to 10% of the outstanding balance annually without any charge. This can be in the form of a single annual payment or a series of regular or irregular payments.

In this example, you could pay a one-off £24,000 payment, a regular monthly overpayment on your normal mortgage payment of up to £2,000 per month or you could pay, say, a single payment of £12,000 plus an extra £1,000 per month. The choice would be yours.

If you pay even an additional £1 over and above this redemption-free amount then the mortgage company will charge you a penalty of 5.0% of the amount being repaid over and above the £20,000 penalty-free amount. For example, if you chose to make a one-off payment of £25,000 then the first £20,000 would be free of redemption penalty and the remaining £5,000 would suffer an early redemption penalty of £250 (£5,000 x 5.0% penalty).

The mortgage company will still allow you to make this larger overpayment. It means that they will only allocate £4,750 of the additional overpayment over and above the £20,000 to your mortgage account. The other £250 goes into the bank's coffers.

Shopping around

As with many financial areas (bank accounts, insurance, paying energy bills, etc.) there is considerable evidence that many people forget that there is a commodity element to paying for a mortgage.

What does this mean? You have costs and those costs could vary from company to company, lender to lender, and so on. **One of the easiest ways of paying down your mortgage early is, in fact, to reduce your costs – if at all possible.**

When it comes to your lender – **are you sure** you have the best deal?

I accept this is not like buying a bag of sweets. Swapping a mortgage from lender A to lender B can be complex and time-consuming. There can also be switching costs and not all lenders may offer you the mortgage freely on the same overall terms.

Nevertheless, the basic point is still valid: the costs of a mortgage are likely to be considerable and very likely, for many people, to be the biggest cost they incur on anything in their lifetime.

The cost saving – if it can be achieved or found – can easily be measured in the thousands or even tens of thousands of pounds.

It is not really feasible to consider a regular switching of a mortgage. This is generally going to be impractical. But the pendulum should not swing too far the other way either. Too many people stay loyal to their mortgage deal for far too long and miss out on significant potential cost savings as a result.

Regular mortgage reviews, say every five years, should always be conducted to test the competitive level of your current mortgage deal and an active approach to keeping the costs of your mortgage as low as possible should always be in your mind.

If you can cut your interest costs, it will help reduce the mortgage more quickly if you then apply the saving towards accelerating the mortgage repayment by scheduling this saving as an overpayment each month.

Provided the sums stack up (for example, taking into account any added one-off cost of switching to a new deal or re-mortgaging to another lender) paying less for the exact same thing is a free hit. That's why two neighbours both with £250,000 mortgages can have different costs and payments because not all mortgages are at the same level of interest (or overall cost). One might be paying £1,250 per month in interest, another £1,000 per month.

I would always suggest taking some time to review the market to see whether it is in your interest to swap mortgage lenders to get a better deal. If you do not have the time, the inclination or the expertise then pass the job to a professionally qualified financial adviser who will be able to advise you accordingly.

Overpayments in practice

Let's have a look now at the effect of these overpayments. Let's start with a £250,000 loan on a capital and interest repayment basis.

Your £250,000 mortgage with no overpayments

(assuming an interest rate of 4.0% per annum that stays the same throughout the term)

- Over the term of the mortgage you would pay around £1,319 per month.
- Over the term of the mortgage you would pay a total of £395,712 in capital and interest payments.
- At the end of the mortgage term the loan is guaranteed to be repaid.

(Table on Page 60)

YEAR	WITHOUT OVERPAYMENT
0	£250,000
1	£244,053
2	£237,865
3	£231,424
4	£224,722
5	£217,746
6	£210,487
7	£202,932
8	£195,070
9	£186,887
10	£178,372
11	£169,510
12	£160,288
13	£150,690
14	£140,701
15	£130,306
16	£119,488
17	£108,229
18	£96,513
19	£84,319
20	£71,629
21	£58,423
22	£44,679
23	£30,376
24	£15,491
25	£0

Figure 1 £250,000 mortgage with no overpayments

Your £250,000 mortgage with a £300 per month overpayment (assuming an interest rate of 4.0% per annum that stays the same throughout the term)

YEAR	WITHOUT OVERPAYMENT	WITH £300 per month OVERPAYMENT
0	£250,000	£250,000
1	£244,053	£240,387
2	£237,865	£230,382
3	£231,424	£219,970
4	£224,722	£209,135
5	£217,746	£197,858
6	£210,487	£186,123
7	£202,932	£173,910
8	£195,070	£161,200
9	£186,887	£147,972
10	£178,372	£134,206
11	£169,510	£119,880
12	£160,288	£104,971
13	£150,690	£89,455
14	£140,701	£73,308
15	£130,306	£56,503
16	£119,488	£39,015
17	£108,229	£20,814
18	£96,513	£1,873
19	£84,319	£0
20	£71,629	£0
21	£58,423	£0
22	£44,679	£0
23	£30,376	£0
24	£15,491	£0
25	£0	£0

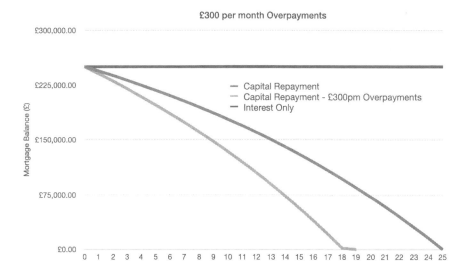

Source: Money Saving Expert

- Over the term of the mortgage you would pay around £1,319 per month.
- By paying an extra £300 on top of the normal mortgage payment each month you would be mortgage free 6 years and 10 months early.
- This would save you around £44,000 in interest payments.
- Over the term of the mortgage you would pay a total of £351,593 in capital and interest payments.

Your £250,000 mortgage with a £500 per month overpayment (assuming an interest rate of 4.0% per annum that stays the same throughout the term)

YEAR	WITHOUT OVERPAYMENT	WITH £ 500 per month OVERPAYMENT
0	£250,000	£250,000
1	£244,053	£237,942
2	£237,865	£225,394
3	£231,424	£212,335
4	£224,722	£198,744
5	£217,746	£184,600
6	£210,487	£169,880
7	£202,932	£154,562
8	£195,070	£138,620
9	£186,887	£122,029
10	£178,372	£104,763
11	£169,510	£86,794
12	£160,288	£68,094
13	£150,690	£48,632
14	£140,701	£28,379
15	£130,306	£7,301
16	£119,488	£0
17	£108,229	£0
18	£96,513	£0
19	£84,319	£0
20	£71,629	£0
21	£58,423	£0
22	£44,679	£0
23	£30,376	£0
24	£15,491	£0
25	£0	£0

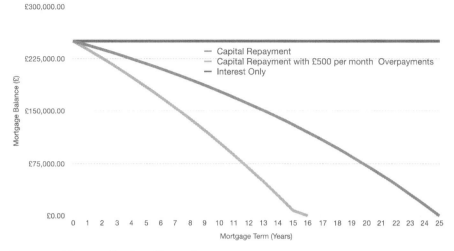

Source: Money Saving Expert

- Over the term of the mortgage you would pay around £1,319 per month.
- By paying an extra £500 on top of the normal mortgage payment each month you would be mortgage free 9 years and 7 months early.
- This would save you around £61,000 in interest payments.
- Over the term of the mortgage you would pay a total of £334,800 in capital and interest payments.

Your £250,000 mortgage with a £50,000 one-off payment and £300 per month overpayment

Now let's assume that you inherited £50,000 three years after taking out the same loan which you chose to immediately pay off the mortgage. In addition you have committed to a £300 per month overpayment (assuming an interest rate of 4.0% per annum that stays the same throughout the term)

- Over the term of the mortgage you would pay around £1,319 per month.
- By paying an extra £300 on top of the normal mortgage payment plus an additional £50,000 one-off lump sum you would be mortgage free 11 years and 2 months early.
- This would save you around £77,700 in interest payments. Over the term of the mortgage you would pay a total of £318,000 in capital and interest payments.

Figure 2 £250,000 mortgage with a £50,000 one-off payment and £300 per month overpayment

YEAR	WITHOUT OVERPAYMENT	WITH £ 50,000 ONE OFF PAYMENT & £300 per month overpayment
0	£250,000	£250,000
1	£244,053	£240,387
2	£237,865	£230,382
3	£231,424	£219,970
4	£224,722	£157,273
5	£217,746	£143,885
6	£210,487	£129,953
7	£202,932	£115,454
8	£195,070	£100,365
9	£186,887	£84,661
10	£178,372	£68,319
11	£169,510	£51,311
12	£160,288	£33,611
13	£150,690	£15,191
14	£140,701	£0
15	£130,306	£0
16	£119,488	£0
17	£108,229	£0
18	£96,513	£0
19	£84,319	£0
20	£71,629	£0
21	£58,423	£0
22	£44,679	£0
23	£30,376	£0
24	£15,491	£0
25	£0	£0

Source: Money Saving Expert

Figure 3 £250,000 mortgage with a £50,000 one-off payment and £300 per month overpayment

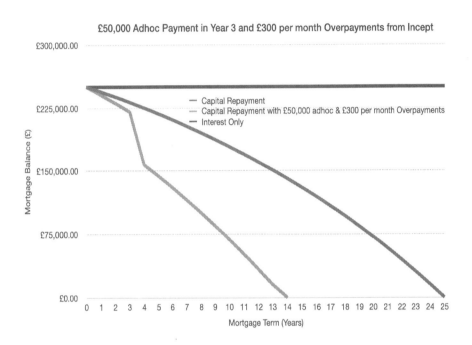

Source: Money Saving Expert

Chapter 11 - Ways to pay off your mortgage early: voluntarily increase your monthly payment

As described in earlier chapters, how your mortgage is actually structured has an important bearing on how you might start to tackle paying it off early.

The most common method of repaying a mortgage is to arrange it on a **capital repayment basis**. If your mortgage is on this basis, you can accelerate the repayment to great effect by voluntarily overpaying month by month or by making random 'one-off' lump sum payments – with the outcome that you directly utilise the so-called reverse compounding we covered in a previous chapter.

Let's look at this again and make some fresh points to help if, indeed, this is the position you are in or if you are looking at this as a viable method.

Your mortgage is likely to be structured around a set term, which could have started some time ago, let's assume a 25-year mortgage term from 2005. You had a mortgage amount at the outset, let's say £200,000 and you are paying the mortgage on a variable interest basis of currently 5.0% per year. You are currently paying £1,169 per month.

Your mortgage has now reduced to £126,533 and you are due to clear the mortgage in full in 2030.

Your personal financial situation will hopefully have improved since you first took the mortgage out and you are now able to significantly overpay the mortgage each month. Let's say that you can afford to pay £3,000 per month. You decide to do so.

In this instance you would be able to clear your mortgage in about four years, that is about nine years early. You pay a total of £144,000 approximately over the next four years and the mortgage is cleared. Had you carried on as normal you would have paid £182,000 approximately so the effect of the overpayment is to save £38,000 in interest payments in total – not bad!

However, it is not that simple. You have to weigh up what else you could do with the money both before and after the overpayment period.

For example, for four years you 'lose out' by paying an extra £1,831 per month which you put towards the mortgage, then for the next nine years you 'gain' that £1,169 per month that you've been paying for so long.

The problem is the 'loss' is in the early years and the 'gain' in the later years. That means the value of the loss is likely to be relatively higher than the value of the gain, due to compounding and inflation.

My point is a simple one – the mathematical calculation is not straightforward. You cannot simply compare two total costs and deduct one from the other.

And this is always the case for anyone in a position of looking at both the true value of paying off a mortgage and how to do so. The maths is not as simple as they look!

I lose no sight of my earlier argument that there is more to this than figures. The psychological aspect of clearing a mortgage and the financial discipline it involves are powerful factors in their own right. However, for the moment we are looking solely at the figures and the structure.

The straight-line comparison between the full term being used and overpaying to bring the term down does not produce a reliable straight-line saving for the reasons outlined.

The complexities do not end there. Using our example above, what is the full financial position of our mortgagee? If they are a very high earner their net financial position as a result of doing things differently, either paying to the full mortgage term or clearing the mortgage earlier, could have very different net tax outcomes.

For example, assume the mortgagee is a director of his or her own company and can dictate their own pay level and also how they are paid.

To overpay the mortgage by £1,831 per month (i.e. increasing the capital repayment) they need a higher level of remuneration, which would be very likely taxed at a higher rate.

Even though the company can afford to pay this increased level of salary, it may be tax inefficient to do so and it may also be more tax efficient or more sensible that the money could be retained in the company in some way for a more tax-efficient payout later.

Where the money comes from to make such an overpayment can have knock-on tax effects in other areas of your life and this could make a significant difference to the true cost of any saving made by overpayment.

If you pay down your mortgage do you then negate the need for a related life assurance policy or serious illness policy? If you do and you no longer need to pay out to protect the mortgage, you can probably count the monthly cost savings on the policies in your overall calculations.

You should also probably consider what you may be able to do when the mortgage has been completely repaid. On a financial planning basis this might involve funding higher pension contributions or generally investing and saving more. On a personal basis it may allow you to travel more, retire early or perhaps help the family financially. For others clearing the mortgage might well allow you to go and buy a more expensive property, take another mortgage and start the whole cycle all over again!

All of this highlights an incredibly important couple of points:

> *You should never judge the saving purely on the straight-line comparison. You have to look at the whole picture and you need to compare and contrast the structure of overpaying using different methods, spreading the view across all your finances. Any adviser or expert who tells you that you save X if you overpay, simply by deducting one of the total figures from the other, is misleading you (probably!).*

There are more aspects to this which you should be aware of – these points by and large apply to all overpayment options:

- You have to be very wary of mortgage terms and conditions. For example, if you are on a fixed rate of interest, are you even able to overpay during the fixed rate period?
- Is overpaying on a capital repayment mortgage in some way going to affect future terms on the mortgage? Some lenders tier their interest rate offerings based on the 'loan to value' of the

mortgage – this being the percentage lent on a property. So, for instance, if you have a 95% mortgage on a property you may actually pay a higher level of interest than if you only owed 50% of the value of the property. Will overpaying your mortgage take your mortgage into a new tier of lending where potentially you could negotiate a better rate of interest when your existing terms have reached the end of their redemption period?

- If you overpay now, can you reduce your payments back down again at a later stage and, if so, on what terms, how often and how much notice will the mortgage company need to make these changes?

- If you need money later for, say, home improvements, can you 'borrow back' these overpayments at the same terms as the original mortgage or will you have to reapply for an additional loan at potentially higher rates of interest?

- How does overpaying now relate to a change in circumstances further down the line, which leads to you wanting to increase the overall mortgage amount borrowed?

That last bullet point is an interesting one to highlight. Let's go back to our example: you have £126,533 owing today on your original £200,000 mortgage. You decide to increase your monthly repayments to £3,000 per month. But then two years later – bang! The company that you own runs into trouble, the property market collapses and interest rates rise. You need £50,000 to stave off the cash flow crisis in the company. You go to your lender and request a £50,000 increase on your mortgage. They refuse.

If you had not overpaid each month and stuck to the original terms and conditions and payment amount, you would have been able to save up (separately, away from the mortgage) well over £40,000, if you had put the 'overpayments' into a separate savings account. Now that's not quite the £50,000 that you want for your business now, but it is not too far off.

The overall position is therefore not just about the savings, even taking into account all the financial aspects, but it is also about how the terms and conditions may affect you and restrict or change future options available to you. Remember the earlier chapter about the past and the future? You do not know what may happen, either in the wider world or the narrower one of your personal circumstances. Any decision you take to overpay your mortgage and/or structure an early repayment has to carefully consider how you may in the future alter the terms IN EVERY WAY.

There are some key points here which actually suggest that simply 'upping' your monthly payments on a capital repayment mortgage could be a false economy and this may not be the most efficient or flexible way to proceed. It is always going to be based on your individual circumstances, but be wary – what may seem straightforward may not be!

Even for those of you with capital repayment mortgages, the other ways of paying off your mortgage early, which we will now look at, are equally as viable as they are for people with interest only mortgages as I will now try and explain.

You do not **have to** overpay your capital repayment mortgage to pay off your mortgage early – you can use the other options as an alternative if this seems better.

Chapter 12 - Ways to pay off your mortgage early: use an offset arrangement

I have often found it difficult to understand why more people do not use offset mortgages in their quest to repay the loan on their home as early and as quickly as possible. When used properly and with sensible terms applied, offset mortgages can help you significantly reduce a mortgage balance. This leads to potentially lower costs over the mortgage term – and/or will reduce the term of the mortgage, which is, after all, the objective.

Let's start by looking at how they work. It is worth noting that there are many variations on the methodology applied from lender to lender, but the following is a broad-brush explanation which will give you the basic idea.

Offset mortgages operate by linking a mortgage account to a secondary bank savings account or a banking current account.

If you borrow via an offset – as with any mortgage – you will be offered a term and a rate of interest, which could be fixed or variable, and this will be the basic structure of your mortgage account.

As an example, let us simplify and assume you borrow £200,000 over 25 years and the interest rate is 5.0% per year.

Instead of setting up a capital repayment mortgage you enter into an 'interest only offset arrangement' and you will need to pay £833.33 per month to the mortgage lender in the normal way made up as follows:

£200,000 x 5.0% per year = £10,000 per year = £833.33 per month

Any cash or deposit account savings that you have are then held in a separate savings account element of the offset mortgage, which is part of the overall offset mortgage arrangement.

Let's assume that you have £20,000 in savings that you keep in this savings account element.

For every day the £20,000 is held in the offset mortgage savings account it is used to reduce the mortgage balance by the net amount or difference between the loan value (£200,000) and the savings value (£20,000) and you are therefore only charged interest on the difference, in this instance being £180,000.

If your mortgage interest is calculated on a daily basis (which most lenders do these days) then your monthly payment would be calculated at something like:

£200,000 loan less £20,000 savings = £180,000 x 5.0% interest / 365 days = £24.66 per day interest. If this savings or bank account balance fluctuates on a day-to-day basis then this daily interest charge will change daily. Your mortgage interest at the end of the month will be calculated as the total number of days in the month multiplied by the daily interest calculation.

The reality is that most people have fluctuating savings amounts so the figure may not stay the same and can go up or down as your savings value fluctuates as you add to it or withdraw from it. The interest will always be calculated on a daily basis (although check the terms on any specific deal).

Therefore you are paying a static monthly mortgage figure – in this example £833.33 per month – as if your mortgage amount is actually £200,000. However, the reality is that you are only being charged on the net amount between this figure and whatever amount you have in savings. Assuming your savings were always £20,000 throughout a year when the interest rate is 5.0%, then you are paying £10,000 in 'interest' payments but actually only being charged £9,000 (5.0% annual interest on £180,000 (£200,000 loan less £20,000 savings)).

The extra £1,000 paid to the mortgage company has the effect of reducing the mortgage balance. It is effectively a very efficient overpayment.

A variation on this is where the offset mortgage is linked to a banking current account and not a savings account. In this instance you would have your £200,000 mortgage facility but now you would use the current account to offset the costs of the interest.

Imagine you are paid £2,500 per month (net of tax). This is paid into your current account on payday and you spend it evenly throughout the month. The positive balance that exists for most of the month is used to offset against the mortgage balance and you are only charged on the difference.

This may sound like pennies but the reality is that by paying interest against an assumed full mortgage balance, but actually only being charged against a smaller balance, even if it is only slightly smaller, the accumulative savings over long periods can be quite astonishing.

> *Even a small amount of savings can make a big difference – a modest ongoing bank account balance of £2,500 could shorten a £100,000 offset mortgage by seven months over a 25-year term!*

There are numerous instances where people with mortgages often have significant sums in savings but don't put two and two together and work out that they can use this to help with their mortgage.

For example, think of Jim, a self-employed builder employing six workers and doing very well for himself. In his 'business bank account' Jim typically holds £50,000 in cash, a combination of money held for a rainy day and future tax payments. He has a £250,000 mortgage. His business bank account pays interest of 0.1% per year, and yet his mortgage costs him 4.2% per year.

If Jim could reorganise his mortgage to an offset arrangement and link the £ 50,000 savings account to the mortgage so that the balance in his savings reduces the amount of interest charged on his mortgage, he would potentially be far better off.

Look at the two figures – 4.2% cost of borrowing and 0.1% benefit of saving. That's 4.1% difference. By reorganising to an offset arrangement Jim can have the benefit of using this capital to reduce the level of interest that he is paying on his mortgage, effectively reducing his annual interest cost by the difference between the outstanding loan and the amount held in the offset account. Jim can therefore have the benefit of this extra 4.1% interest saving which on £50,000 is potentially worth £2,050 per year.

Rarely though does anyone have a constant savings balance as shown in this example.

If the money is for tax payments, salaries or other capital expenditure within a business then there could be wild swings in the bank account savings value as tax monies are saved up and then paid out when the tax is due or other capital expenditure is made.

Or maybe there is an unexpected windfall from a particularly lucrative job, or conversely suddenly money is needed for some unexpected payment.

None of this matters because the offset mortgage/savings arrangement copes with this and can accommodate this sort of required flexibility.

Most mortgages of this type are going to have significant flexibility involved, which can include allowing you to reduce your sum owing (through the offset mechanism described) but also to increase it again later on down the line should your finances require a boost, without the need for a new mortgage application or having to ask the mortgage company for more money.

Offset mortgages and the various different terms offered by different lenders all work on the same basic principle: **they allow you to use positive balances in other linked bank or deposit accounts which has the effect, day by day, of reducing your mortgage balance, thereby creating an overpayment. This in turn will reduce the term of your mortgage.**

If you are self-employed, or have a high level of disposable income and/or have a high level of cash savings that you do not want to allocate to other investments then an offset mortgage should seriously be considered. It is an extremely efficient way of paying down a mortgage, albeit because of their flexibility they can be slightly more expensive than conventional mortgages and the choice of schemes available can be somewhat limited as few lenders offer them.

Additionally, I have also seen offset mortgages used by property developers and property investors as a simple and convenient 'credit line' facility when investing, refurbishing and then either selling or renting investment property. Once the offset mortgage is in place the flexibility that this type of scheme can offer makes the overall facility extremely attractive.

Chapter 13 - Retirement interest only mortgages

If you have an interest only mortgage then it is highly likely that you will not have anything formally in place with your mortgage lender to clear your mortgage at the end of the term (as opposed to the capital repayment option which is a contract between you and the lender towards the overall and final repayment of the loan).

Let me clarify. It is highly likely that the mortgage company will **demand** repayment of their loan at a set pre-arranged date in the future (normally the end of the mortgage term) – but contractually you may not have anything in place to actually do this. The responsibility for how you repay this mortgage debt is entirely with you. It is highly likely that the mortgage company will take little interest in **how** you intend repaying the mortgage and highly unlikely that they will keep track of your progress over the years.

How you accumulate the monies necessary to clear the mortgage on the agreed repayment date is entirely up to you. It is absolutely **your** responsibility to ensure that one way or another there are sufficient monies available at that set repayment date (or before) because otherwise the mortgage company could potentially force you to sell the property in order to clear the debt.

This widespread problem is potentially a disaster waiting to happen – particularly for the older generation.

The government regulator, the Financial Conduct Authority, has estimated that there are around 1.67 million full interest only and part capital repayment mortgages in the UK. This accounts for around 17.6% of all the outstanding mortgage accounts and over the coming years more and more of these will need repayment.

Remember that prior to 2008 interest only mortgages were commonplace, mortgage borrowings were relatively easy to obtain and there was a 'borrow now, worry about it later mentality'.

The challenge now of course is that many of these mortgages are beginning to come to the end of their mortgage terms and people are beginning to realise that they should have acted far sooner in thinking about repaying their mortgages and are being forced to take drastic steps to repay their borrowings. This could involve selling the property, re-mortgaging to another lender on a repayment basis for a far longer term if affordability allows, or even considering equity release to carry the mortgage debt far into retirement.

At the time of writing the government has realised that there is a serious problem in the making and have encouraged mortgage lenders to offer 'retirement interest only mortgages'. These are very similar to standard interest only mortgages but can run far beyond normal retirement dates. The cost of the mortgage interest still has to be paid in the normal way but the mortgage debt is cleared when the house is sold, or when the mortgage holder goes into long-term care or when the mortgage holder passes away.

Mortgage lenders will always have to be sure that customers are able to afford the commitment of servicing a retirement interest only (RIO) mortgage. Customers with poor levels of retirement income are likely to be refused a RIO in the interests of all concerned. Lenders have also been told that 'When assessing the affordability of a RIO with joint borrowers, the firm should consider the ability of a single borrower to continue making the required payments if the other dies, taking into account relevant evidence such as pensions payable to the surviving spouse or civil partner.'

At the time of writing, RIO mortgages are still in their relative infancy. They potentially could be available to borrowers over the age 55, but it is more likely that the ages of 60 to 65 will be more commonplace. In addition to this loans are likely to be restricted to 60% of the value of the property and the actual loan amounts limited in value. This will evidently cause issues for anyone with a higher level of borrowing on their property and with retirement fast approaching.

It is highly advisable that any individual coming up to retirement who has not repaid their interest only mortgage and does not have the resources to do so should take professional advice to ensure that all of their options are considered. Among these options will be the subject of equity release which we will discuss in the next chapter.

Chapter 14 - Equity Release

Equity release is a means of releasing funds from the ownership of a property in retirement. It provides the advantage of requiring no liability or commitment to repay any interest charged by the equity release provider on an ongoing basis, or to pay off any capital at any time before the property is sold or the property owner goes into care. It is a special type of arrangement which can only be accessed by the over 55s and in the case of a couple where the younger of the couple is aged 55 or over.

How does it work? Equity release is the overall term used that describes the release of equity held in a property in a single cash payment or in a series of payments over a period of time.

In reality there are fundamentally two types of scheme: 'lifetime mortgages' and 'home reversion plans'. These schemes both achieve the objective of releasing equity for the retired homeowner but are actually very different.

A **lifetime mortgage** is exactly as it says: a mortgage or loan for the rest of your life, however long that may be. Any interest charged on the mortgage by the lender comes with no obligation to make ANY payments, as the interest 'rolls up' and increases the loan outstanding. The loan is then repaid when the property is sold, which will either be when the owner goes into care (full-time residential care – not care in the home) or passes away. In the case of a married couple living in the property, it is when this event – residential care or death – occurs for the second person (this provides the surety that if a spouse goes into care or dies that the property is secured for the rest of the surviving spouse's life) that the property will be sold.

There are some lifetime mortgages which come with an option to make interest payments if the homeowner so wishes. Thus there are variations on the structure of the basic scheme from lender to lender.

A **home reversion plan** is quite different. In this case the owner(s) sells a portion or percentage of their property to a 'home reversion provider', not a mortgage or equity release lender. There is no loan involved at all. The home reversion provider purchases a percentage (or all) of the value of the property for a single cash lump sum but provides a lifetime guarantee that the homeowner can live there for the rest of their days.

The owners, having sold a percentage of the value of their property to the home reversion provider, then live in the property as before (there is no rent payable on the percentage they have sold) until, as above, they either go into residential care or die.

At this point the property is sold and the remaining property proceeds are divided up between the owner's estate and the home reversion provider depending on the individual percentages owned by each party.

So the first scheme involves borrowing while the second involves actually selling a share of the property that you live in.

This book is not about whether equity release is the right option, nor about which scheme might work better in different circumstances. My objective within these pages is to help you identify ways of paying off your mortgage, and pay it off early if at all possible. In this respect equity release is a viable option in some cases, particularly for retired homeowners who are left with some outstanding mortgage debt.

Many people are suspicious of equity release as there have been many very well publicised problems with this form of lending in the past. Many will think that having an equity release is just swapping one form of mortgage debt on a property for another, or that selling a bit of the house to release cash is tantamount to the same thing.

That's a fair point. However, there are substantial differences between equity release and a conventional mortgage which mean that it does have a place within many scenarios. The differences are:

- Most conventional mortgages cannot run beyond certain age limits.
- Equity release is a way of releasing funds for common retirement needs in a structured fashion which a conventional mortgage would not be able to support.
- There is no obligation to make interest payments and no need to pay rent to a third-party landlord.
- Current equity release schemes are now highly regulated and have many types of safeguards attached to ensure that the homeowner's interests are protected at all times which a conventional mortgage does not have. (For example, an equity release provider can never force the sale of a property if the owner is still living there and the value of the equity release loan can never exceed the value of the property.)

These differences can lead to many situations where it is feasible to use equity release in later life, where this is deemed to make financial sense for an individual's or couple's needs.

Equity release must always be secured against an unencumbered property, i.e. one that does not have a loan or mortgage secured against it. But it is possible to pay off a residual outstanding mortgage (or other loan) as part of the equity release package at the outset.

For example, if you had £30,000 outstanding on a mortgage and a property valued at £400,000, you may be able to release £100,000 from an equity release scheme. This would free up £70,000, not £100,000, to be used as freely as you like, as the £30,000 difference would be used to clear the existing conventional mortgage.

The structural differences of an equity release and its suitability as a tool to use in retirement means there will be plenty of situations where shifting from a traditional mortgage to equity release would make a lot of sense. In this respect equity release is a viable option in the range of choices when it comes to clearing off a mortgage.

A further consideration for retired mortgaged homeowners is one of the new 'retirement interest only mortgages' which were discussed in an earlier chapter.

For more details on the subject of Equity Release, please see our other publication – 'The Astute Guide to Equity Release' by Darren Fisher which is available on Amazon and other online book stores.

Chapter 15 - Other tips for paying off your mortgage

After having had a mortgage for a few years consider re-mortgaging to a shorter term

The only constant in life is that most things change over time. You might be in the fortunate position of having a substantial pay rise, or because of having raised a family you go from having one salary to two. Or perhaps you've started a business which over time has become successful and you are in a position to afford a bigger home, or perhaps you have simply adopted some of the other earlier mortgage-reducing plans that we have discussed in this book and you are now in a position where you can pay off the mortgage in another ten years by simply re-mortgaging.

Let's say you have a 25-year fixed rate mortgage for £300,000 at an interest rate of 4.5% per annum. Five years later, you refinance into a ten-year loan at 4.0% per annum. Doing so pays off the mortgage 15 years earlier and saves you tens of thousands of pounds in mortgage interest and capital repayments.

In considering re-mortgaging to a lower term you must remember that this is likely to come at some level of initial cost. There may be property revaluation fees, existing mortgage redemption costs, legal fees and mortgage arrangement fees that may have to paid in order for you to change lender. All of this needs to be taken into consideration when changing from one mortgage lender to another and you have to build these costs into the cost of the overall mortgage. You also have to be very aware that a quicker payoff means substantially higher monthly payments. This is fine for as long as you have that much higher income or your partner has returned to work but you also need to give some thought as to how you would afford these extra payments if something goes wrong. What happens if you or your partner loses their job or becomes pregnant or your business has a downturn? Mortgage companies are not the most humane of organisations and they have little patience for people's problems – the bottom line is that you must never forget that all the mortgage company is interested in is getting their money! As long as you pay them each month without any problems they will leave you alone.

Remember that if you re-mortgage to a lower term and therefore agree to increased payments you must be able to manage your finances and maintain payments in the bad times as well as the good!

Make one extra mortgage payment each year

Instead of committing yourself to reducing the actual mortgage term and paying substantially more each month, which may in itself be unsustainable in the long term – particularly if you are self-employed or have an insecure employment arrangement – then consider 'stashing some cash' into a savings account over the course of the year and then make one extra payment each year, say at Christmas or on your birthday.

How about committing to a short-term savings arrangement for six or twelve months and saving, say, £300 per month into a cash savings account? Once you have built up a few thousand pounds and are happy to do so then make arrangements to pay this off the mortgage. The effect may be small overall but the rosy feeling you will have having taken a positive step will make the sacrifice worthwhile!

It doesn't really matter how much you set aside, whether it be tens, hundreds or thousands of pounds each month, as you will be committing emotionally and practically to repaying your mortgage.

Windfall money

Any little win in life is a bonus, whether it's a tax refund, a small inheritance or a bonus at work. Once you have established that you have never had this money in the first place and that you don't actually need to commit this 'windfall money' to other areas (and I am sure that there are many potential uses of such money) then consider utilising this as a one-off payment against your mortgage.

Let's assume that you have a 25-year fixed-rate mortgage for £150,000 at an interest rate of 4.5%. Five years later, your great aunt sadly passes away and you inherit £10,000. After having considered your wider finances and having checked the terms and conditions of your existing mortgage (beware redemption charges!) you then decide to use this £10,000 inheritance as a one-off single overpayment on your mortgage. This will potentially save you up to £9,000 in mortgage interest over the remaining term of the mortgage.

Internet banking

Now I approach this particular section with a little trepidation because at the time of writing in early 2019 Internet banking is a relatively reliable form of banking platform, although it is not without its problems. High-street bank branches are diminishing at an alarming rate and I am pretty sure that within a few years most will have disappeared as reliance on the Internet, and particularly mobile apps, becomes more and more prevalent. Banks seem to be courting the Internet savvy, and particularly the all-embracing phone-wielding millennials who will think nothing of running their entire lives on their iPhones, while at the same time showing scant thought or respect to the older generation who feel that having a local branch to go to is actually a really good thing.

But Internet banking from a mortgage repayment perspective is potentially a good thing. For example, IF – and this may be a big IF – your mortgage lender has managed to drag itself into the Internet age, then it may be possible to link your existing mortgage account to your main bank current account via Internet banking.

To do this you will simply need to find your specific account number and sort code that are linked to your individual mortgage account, and then link them to your Internet banking. It is quite likely that modern high-street lenders or their subsidiaries will be able to give you this information but you might struggle with the smaller, specialist lenders such as those specialising in poor credit (adverse credit)' or buy-to-let mortgage lenders or those lenders that have miraculously appeared over the years having bought the debt of other mortgage companies and that are now administering this debt at probably higher mortgage rates.

So with a little questioning, if you can obtain an account number and sort code for your mortgage, you can then try and link them directly to your Internet banking in the normal way. Then in the same way as you pay your normal bills using your day-to-day banking whether that be council tax, utility bills, insurance, etc. – just arrange to send your mortgage company a very small payment – let's say in the first instance £20.

It may be that your mortgage company will allow you to access your mortgage online, if they offer this facility than make arrangements to access your mortgage account via their website. Go to the transactions list and if this errant £20 payment appears in the list of transactions then you have successfully linked your bank account to your main mortgage account and can then make unscheduled, occasional and irregular payments at will. Happy days!

Should you not be able to access your mortgage account online I would suggest that you give your mortgage company a call and ask them to check your recent transactions and see whether they have received an additional £20 payment. If that is the case then again, happy days! You are in a position where you can now make occasional, sporadic irregular payments to your mortgage account as the mood takes you.

Now let's assume that you and your family go out for dinner once a week and spend, say, £100 in doing so. One week you get invited over by the in-laws and find that you do not have to pay for dinner out that week and indeed find yourself £100 better off. Use your Internet banking to pay that additional £100 off your mortgage! Do that once a month for a year and you've paid an extra £1,200 off your mortgage – on top of any other overpayments or other single payments that you might be paying off your mortgage.

Now I realise that having an extra £100 saved from not going out to dinner can be spent on a thousand or more things elsewhere but this is actually a really good use of this money. You would have spent it anyway, so why not pay it off the mortgage? You might have gone out another evening, but perhaps you might not have, so pay it off the mortgage anyhow!

Linking a mortgage to your Internet banking is a really easy way to pay occasional, sporadic payments as well as larger one-off payments when circumstances allow. I have actually heard of someone 'fining themselves' for checking their Internet banking to the tune of £20 every time they do so and using this amount to help pay down the mortgage. He checked his bank balance on average four times a week so was paying off an extra £80 a week by voluntarily making these occasional overpayments. That's nearly £1,000 a year in overpayments!

Now when doing this remember the rule about redemption penalties and the potential costs that your mortgage company might invoke on you when making these payments. This only really works if the mortgage company embraces flexible, without cost payment practices and will not charge you for these extra payments. Check the terms and conditions of your mortgage before you embark on this particular route!

Lump sums, windfalls and inheritances

It is interesting to Google 'should I pay off my mortgage early?' or something similar and read some of the articles this throws up. As with many similar types of Google search what you find is just as likely to give rise to more questions and confusion than provide any sensible or conclusive answers.

I mention this now simply because for a lot of people this question comes into view if they suddenly receive a significant lump sum, perhaps from an inheritance, a gift from a family member or an unexpected windfall.

There is a difference between formulating a well defined savings or investment strategy in advance to clear a mortgage early and the opportunity which can arise one day if a sudden windfall lands in your lap.

Let us return to the Google search. I would suggest the replies are roughly split equally between 'experts' suggesting you should use money received as a lump to clear off your mortgage and those who say you shouldn't.

In the end, it doesn't matter too much because in a way both arguments are right, in the sense that there are good reasons to clear a mortgage and good reasons not to if you suddenly have the opportunity presented by a windfall.

It is going to depend entirely on circumstances – your situation, plus your lifestyle, family and financial goals. These will determine the answer and even then it won't be the 'right' answer all the time.

The right answer can only be known with the benefit of time and hindsight. You have to make decisions as you see fit at the time, so you can only make judgement calls when the opportunity arises.

Whether you pay off or partially pay off a mortgage or not with a windfall is a very personal judgement call. Let's say your basic situation is that you currently have a £100,000 mortgage outstanding and you receive an inheritance of £100,000.

If the mortgage is costing you 5.0% per year in interest charges and you use the inheritance to clear the mortgage, you save at least

£5,000 per year in interest costs and now don't have to worry about any of the other costs associated with the mortgage.

So if you don't pay off the mortgage you need to be fairly sure that the value of holding the £100,000 in some other investment or spending it some other way is better value than the mortgage costs you would have otherwise saved.

However, you cannot know that outcome for sure in advance. You might be able to look back at some point and know, but that is the nature of all things financial and investment related.

Instead of using the money to pay off the mortgage you might decide to use it to help your children with their education costs or assist them in getting onto the housing ladder themselves. How do you measure this level of parental assistance in monetary terms?

Or you might use the £100,000 to start a new business – this might work and again it might not in the long run. The business could go bust or over time could turn into a multi-million pound enterprise.

You might want to go on a series of holidays for a number of years using the windfall to help pay for them. What's the value of the enhancement and quality of life versus paying off the mortgage? Indeed how do we measure the pleasure derived from pursuing different options?

As common themes throughout this book, all of these factors have far more than just a straight mathematical comparison attached to them. If you are in a position where you have an unexpected windfall, maybe from selling some shares in a company, from an inheritance or from any other source then using this to pay off a mortgage, either in whole or in part, has exactly the same dynamic attached as any other.

You should look closely at your entire financial and tax position, consider your lifestyle and financial goals, and then formulate a plan accordingly which will suit your own circumstances.

That is why Google cannot produce a convincing answer either way – because the answer lies in your own financial planning and in your own dreams and aspirations.

Chapter 16 - Using investment products to repay a mortgage

This chapter will quickly discuss the basic principles of using investment products to repay your mortgage but the likelihood is that you will need to seek professional financial planning advice to ensure that you have the most suitable option for your personal needs.

This is a really big subject and one which I will attempt to summarise as best I can but there are a few basic points that you need to consider first. Let's begin by explaining that the world of saving and investing can be very simply split into three main groups:

- **Short-term savings (or 'emergency funds')** – made up of bank and building society cash deposit savings accounts, cash ISAs, National Savings, etc.;
- **Medium-term investments (five to ten years in duration)** – made up of unit trusts and equity individual savings accounts among many others;
- **Long-term investments (ten years or more in duration)** – such as personal pensions, final salary pension schemes, workplace pensions, again among many others.

Using the same example as the one used in an earlier chapter, let us assume you took out a £200,000 interest only mortgage in 2005 and have to clear this by 2030, as your mortgage term was for 25 years.

If it had been a capital repayment mortgage, you would have had higher monthly payments to pay to the lender (as you would have been obliged to pay capital and interest, not just interest) which would have had the effect of reducing the amount owed today (2019) to roughly £126,533.

However, if you had had an interest only mortgage you still owe the lender today the full £200,000. Hopefully you will have saved up these £42,000 extra mortgage savings under payments somewhere otherwise you will not 'be on target' and in serious danger of not having sufficient funds to repay your mortgage at the end of the term.

So if you are going to use these extra payments to build capital over the long term to repay your mortgage, where do you invest them? Let's look at the options available to you.

Deposit savings accounts

In my opinion, this is probably the least sensible route to consider due to the very low rates of interest that cash deposits yield (Remember the 'Short Term' argument above). Banks, building societies and other lenders are more than happy to accept your cash deposits, pay you a very low rate of interest – let's say 1.25% per annum and then lend it back out to you again in the form of a mortgage at a rate of say, 5.0% per annum. At the time of writing this chapter in early 2019, the highest yielding instant access deposit account was paying around 1.50% per annum.

At the same time, the rate of inflation has risen to 2.50% per annum so effectively the 'true value' of having money on deposit is actually minus 1.0% per annum – in its truest sense you are actually losing money each year by having money on deposit.

The other consideration with saving money in bank and building society accounts is that the money is accessible. Speaking from experience, over the years there will bound to be financial emergencies where money is needed for something – and the last thing you really want to do is to be dipping into the mortgage repayment pot. If you do, experience tells me that it will be very difficult for you to get yourself ahead again and replace these lost funds.

As I have already intimated it is very important to have easily accessible emergency money put aside for those times when money is needed quickly and deposit accounts are absolutely fine for this – but any professional adviser would not recommend using bank and building society cash deposit accounts for building a long term savings pot.

Individual Savings Accounts

Over the years many people and advisers have favoured the use of individual savings accounts (ISAs) to accumulate the sums necessary to pay their mortgage off on the due date (or before – ideally!).

Let us firstly quickly explain the main types of ISA that are available in the marketplace:

- **Cash ISAs** – invest only in cash deposits, and by their nature tend to yield low rates of bank or building society interest generally in line with other cash deposits of a similar nature.
- **Equity ISAs** – provide substantially greater investment choice including investing in stocks and shares (in the UK and

internationally), fixed interest holdings including gilts and corporate bonds, commercial property and cash deposits.

There are also 'innovative ISAs', 'lifetime ISAs' and 'junior ISAs' which are available. For the purposes of repaying a mortgage I will concentrate here on the use of equity ISAs which are by far the most commonly used ISA investment used to build capital over the long term.

ISAs, if used correctly, are potentially excellent tools for building capital over the long term. They are regulated by the Financial Conduct Authority and it is Her Majesty's government that provides contribution limits, the rules regarding investment and the excellent long-term tax benefits that are available when investing in an ISA. **However**, putting together a strategy for repaying a mortgage needs professional financial planning advice and we would always suggest that anyone thinking of building an ISA or other savings/investment portfolio to repay a mortgage should take such advice first.

The reason for this is that there is a huge choice of investment options available to an individual seeking to build a long-term mortgage repayment pot. These differing investment options carry varying levels of investment returns and associated levels of investment risk. For example, ISAs allow you to invest in cash deposits which yield low rates of interest but which carry correspondingly very low levels of risk. At the other end of the spectrum ISAs can invest in stocks and shares of almost all types, both locally and further afield, which carry dramatically higher levels of risk. Annual investment returns can potentially be much higher than cash based ISAs but the level of risk taken can also be correspondingly higher.

Investment-based equity ISAs also carry higher levels of costs ad these costs need to be taken into consideration when working out how much you need to pay into your ISA in order to ensure that you have enough capital at the end of the term to clear the mortgage.

ISAs are a great savings product to use in this respect for a number of reasons:

- They build up a savings pot free of income and capital gains taxes, thereby providing valuable tax benefits which can help boost investment returns over the long term.
- There are healthy personal allowances with regard to the amounts that can be invested in an ISA each tax year.
- You have great flexibility around how you invest in an ISA, you can make payments at a rate and speed which suits you and if you need the odd payment holiday you can do so without penalty. Payments can be made on an annual or a monthly basis, or as a single or series of single lump sums.
- There are multiple investment options available with an ISA from low-risk investments or funds to ones with higher risk, so they can be adapted to personal circumstances and preferences.
- Likewise you can switch investment funds around within an ISA and choose different funds at different times. For example, in the early years you could invest quite aggressively and if this successful and your investments perform well, you can switch to lower-risk funds to preserve the gains made and the money built up in later years.

- They do seem hardy in political terms. Hopefully they will be here to stay as far as we can foresee and are unlikely to be treated badly by future governments (although nothing is guaranteed in that respect!).

So ISAs really do seem to make sense as the investment vehicle to save your money in and one day repay your mortgage.

Let's return to the previous example. You took out a £200,000 mortgage in 2005 which needs to be repaid in 2030. You owe £200,000 today but you have used ISAs well and you are investing £336 per month ongoing (which you have been doing for the past 13 years). These ISA investments are now worth £76,000 today.

This makes it look like you are a little better off than the capital repayment mortgagee upon which you still owe £126,533 – and in a way you are, because although you owe £200,000, you have £76,000 tucked away into an ISA portfolio so your 'net' position is actually £124,000.

That is the crucial difference between a capital repayment mortgage and an interest only mortgage backed by a savings vehicle (such as an ISA). The way the capital repayment option is structured you speed up the majority of the repayment in the later years as we described earlier, therefore on as much of a like-for-like basis as you can get, an investment equity ISA portfolio tends to compare better the longer you run it.

However, the much more important factor with the ISA option is to understand the investment aspect.

I have quoted a figure above of £76,000 as the accumulated value after 13 years. This assumes £336 has been paid monthly for 13 years and has achieved an investment return – on whatever fund or funds (or other investments or accounts you had used) has returned – of an average of 5.5% per year. This is a return after product charges have been accounted for.

Why £336 per month? This is the amount of the interest cost payable to the lender plus £336 which equals the equivalent capital repayment cost so that we are comparing like for like.

The actual figure is £76,304. But what would it be at different average yearly returns?

These are the different accumulated amounts assuming annual returns (after charges and costs) of:

2.5% per year	£61,861
4.0% per year	£68,602
5.5% per year	£76,304
7.0% per year	£85,119

(All assume £336 per month for the full 13-year term).
These figures are for illustration purposes only.

You will note quite a swing between the figures, especially from the lowest to the highest illustrated. This emphasises how much the ISA route is all about the underlying investment approach taken.

If we stretch this forward to the end of the term you will see the swing escalates greatly (because of the compounding effect):

2.5% per year	£139,835
4.0% per year	£172,748
5.5% per year	£215,725
7.0% per year	£272,184

(All assume £336 per month for the full 25-year term)
These figures are for illustration purposes only.

Notice not only the massive swing of £140,000 or so between the lowest and highest illustrated returns but also the fact that in the lower returns figures you have failed to accumulate enough to clear the mortgage. This is a really important point – an equity ISA mortgage will NOT be GUARANTEED to repay your mortgage at the end of the mortgage term. It is imperative therefore to undertake regular reviews to ensure that your ISA is on track to repay your mortgage. If it is not you may have to make some changes to the way you do things.

Only with the higher returns figures do you have enough to clear your mortgage (with quite a bit extra at 7.0% per year).

This is the key difference between an ISA (and any other type of savings vehicle connected to a mortgage) and a capital repayment mortgage: one is reliant on a savings return, the other is guaranteed to pay off the mortgage to the penny, on the dot.

Now let's say we are in the same situation as before. We have around £76,000 saved up and want to pay off the mortgage as quickly as possible with the extra money we can now put towards it.

The extra £1,831 could now be added to the ISA pot, so we have £76,000 in the ISA today and now increase the monthly payments to £2,167. It would take about 45 months to get to £200,000 if we continued to get 5.5% per year growth, 51 months at 2.5% per year growth and 40 months at 7.0% per year growth. So the growth doesn't actually make that much difference at that level of extra payment.

What this tells you is something very important: if you escalate your monthly payments in this way to clear the mortgage quickly – de-risk!!

Why? Because if you invest aggressively to try and get higher growth you don't make that much difference. On the other hand, a high-risk strategy could lose you money, your invested sum could fall and this would seriously derail you. A negative figure would reduce the £76,000 already built up and put you into reverse.

Whichever way we look at this we can see the true picture: if you use savings vehicles like ISAs, you are using the savings dynamic to pay down your mortgage, good investment returns produce positive results while poor (or negative) returns produce bad results.

The investment option offered by an ISA is a different beast altogether to the safe, reliable and known capital repayment option.

Neither is better than the other. There are different ways to approach the same thing and those differences need to be factored in to personal circumstances and preferences.

Where the ISA does have an advantage, however, is in the flexibility it offers. If we look back to the previous chapter where we considered some 'what if?' scenarios, then we can see the ISA option provides greater flexibility should circumstances change. Using the same example as before, if you find your business suddenly needs money or you have some other form of financial emergency you have not tied the accrued overpayments directly into the main mortgage account and you could use the accrued sum in your ISA for other purposes, not just the mortgage.

It is important to note that ISAs can also be used by capital repayment mortgagees as a means to overpay their mortgage too. Anyone currently using a capital repayment structure who decides to try and accelerate their mortgage repayment can opt to use an ISA as an extension of their structure. Even an additional £100 invested monthly over ten years will take a big chunk out of any mortgage balance. This type of mix and match approach is considered later.

The important part of this to note is that there is no reason why anyone using capital repayment as their primary method of paying their mortgage should be hamstrung by this method if they want to start overpaying. Other options are available than just sending the overpayment to the mortgage company!

To summarise, ISAs are probably the most useful and relevant savings vehicle for most people who want to use an investment-led approach to accumulating sums to clear their mortgage. The combination of tax benefits, multiple investment options and flexibility of payment make them ideal as a mortgage repayment plan, especially when clearing the mortgage early is the aim.

As has been mentioned previously, take professional financial planning advice if considering using an equity ISA to repay your mortgage. The options available to you are extensive. A professional will help you make the correct financial and investment decisions for you, your family and your finances.

Chapter 17 - Using personal pensions

Firstly, some housekeeping before we delve into the subject of pensions. There are many ways to fund a retirement pot but for the purposes of this chapter I am concentrating solely on the private personal pension arrangement and how it could be used in a mortgage repayment scenario. This would perhaps be suitable for a self-employed person or an employee without an occupational final salary pension and purposefully excludes any other form of pension that might be available in the marketplace. This is an extremely complex area and one where professional advice is definitely needed.

Hopefully by this stage of this book I have established that there are really only two ways you can structure a mortgage repayment plan over a long period:

You can either:

- Have a capital interest and repayment mortgage.

Or:

- Have an interest only mortgage with a savings or investment plan running alongside.

There is, of course, a third option which is to do a bit of both.

Previously we have considered the position where the second option was to have an interest only mortgage plus an equity investment ISA plan (or plans) alongside.

The reality is that you can use any form of savings or investment vehicle which you decide will do the job to your very best advantage. This brings into the equation the pension plan option. Should you pour your hard-earned monthly savings into a pension as opposed to an ISA?

To begin to answer this we should go back to a constant theme – everything depends on the circumstances and what is most suitable for one situation could be wrong in another. There are no golden rules or any perfect solution. If in doubt, I repeat, do ensure that you take professional financial planning advice!

Secondly, the debate around ISAs versus pensions almost requires a book all on its own. If you ask ten experts which is the better savings vehicle to use, you will probably get eleven different answers.

Thirdly, it is rarely the case for many savers and mortgagees that the choice boils down to one or the other. Most people paying mortgages also have to give serious consideration as to where their retirement income is going to come from, so the financial planning decision processes have to deal with more than one goal. This probably means in most cases that for the majority of people they will be using ISAs and pensions concurrently in their planning.

However, for the purposes of thinking about paying off a mortgage, let us narrow down the view to a straight comparison. Let's consider what the objective is: it is to get a pot of money together so that a mortgage can be paid off at a future date.

The terms 'ISAs' and 'pensions' describe legal structures that apply to savings vehicles. Provided you get your pot of money together and the legal structure of an ISA/pension does not interfere with your ability to release this pot in your favour, I am guessing you couldn't care less about the legal structures! You just want to maximise the amount of savings you can accumulate in the shortest possible amount of time.

Broadly speaking, whether you invest your money in an ISA and/or a pension is down to your long-term objectives but they do tend to invest in very similar underlying investments.

For example, with both you can invest in investment funds that themselves invest in stocks and shares, fixed-interest instruments, cash, property (but not residential property) and other alternative investments such as commodities. In each case you can buy individual funds investing in certain sectors or you can buy 'risk-graded multi-asset funds' which are favoured by many professionals these days.

There is a slight difference between an ISA and a pension when it comes to investing in property. For example, both allow you to invest in third-party property investment funds, but only a 'self invested personal pension' offers the possibility of investing directly in an individual commercial property. Residential property is not allowed in any circumstance.

So actually investing in pensions and ISAs can be very similar. With both options you need to decide how much investment risk you are prepared to take and then you are able to invest in a variety of investment funds which will suit your purposes and needs.

At this point the similarity between pensions and equity ISAs ends.

It is important to understand that a pension, in whatever form, is meant to provide an income in retirement. At some point you (and your spouse) will likely seek to give up work, put your feet up and actually retire from the world of work. The government are equally keen for you to invest for the future as they basically do not want any more people than absolutely necessary to be reliant on the state benefits system. The government therefore provide very attractive tax benefits for you to invest in pensions, whether they be private arrangements or more commonly used company pensions. These tax benefits can be quite substantial and over the course of many years may be very valuable.

Part of these tax benefits is the ability to take up to a quarter of a pension fund as a single or a series of tax-free lump sums over the period of your retirement. It is likely that if you are thinking of using a pension to repay a mortgage it is this lump sum that will be used to repay the loan.

Since 2015 pensions can be drawn from the age of 55 under new 'Pension Freedom' rules, which in theory means that a person can access their pension fund either partially or in full at any time in almost whatever format they like.

The money in a pension can now be taken how and when the investor chooses. This change made pensions and ISAs more similar than ever. Of course, before age 55 there is a major difference as a pension cannot be accessed whereas an ISA can. But after 55 (when realistically most people will be targeting paying off their mortgage) the full withdrawal levels out ISAs and pensions to a significant extent.

Where there is a huge difference, however, is the way in which pensions and ISAs are taxed at the point of receipt.

- ISAs receive no tax relief on any money paid into them.
- Pensions receive tax relief in various forms applied to the contributions being paid into them.
- ISAs accumulate all money tax free within their structures and allow for all withdrawals to be made from them with no tax being deducted.
- Pensions accumulate all money tax free within their structures but only a quarter of withdrawals are tax free. The remaining three-quarters are taxable at an individual's highest marginal rate of tax in the year of withdrawal.

These are the some of the main differences and we shall see how they affect things in a moment.

Before this it is worth pointing out some other factors which can be relevant:

- The allowances – the maximum amount you can pay into pensions and ISAs – are also very different. ISAs have an annual personal allowance which is not particular to the individual, their income or their tax status. Pension contributions are limited by HMRC and there is a cap on the maximum amount you can build up over an individual's lifetime, whereas an ISA does not have such limitations.

These differences could be very important and I don't want to downplay them, but they are not especially relevant to the broad comparison I wish to make in the context of a mortgage.

Returning to this comparison, we need to simplify by considering the position in terms of the different tax treatments alone:

- Pensions have tax relief applied on contributions, ISAs do not.
- Pensions are taxed on withdrawals (albeit the first 25% is available tax free), ISAs are not taxed on withdrawals.

Let's now look quickly at how payments into an ISA and a pension accumulate over time. For the purpose of this example we are referring to 'Personal Pensions' only rather then any form of workplace based occupational pension.

If you wanted to pay £336 per month into a personal pension as we looked at in the last chapter instead of an ISA, then it will not be £336 being invested each month. You will actually have £420 being invested each month.

That's because, at the time of writing the government very generously apply basic rate tax relief to the amount being paid into the pension. So, the calculation here is that basic rate tax relief of 20% is added at source; £420 x 20% = £84, so you add the £84 to the £336, which is how £420 is actually paid into the pension.

You pay a regular direct debit each month to your pension plan of £336 and £420 actually gets invested. The pension company automatically claims the other £84 from HM Revenue.

However, it may be that due to your circumstances (perhaps you are a carer, or are not able to work due to being disabled or being a house person) you may not be able to pay £336 per month or £420 per month into a pension, as you have insufficient earnings.

The good news is that, at the time of writing, absolutely anyone can pay £3,600 gross of basic rate tax relief per year into a pension (£2,880 net of tax relief plus £720 basic rate tax relief) regardless of their earnings.

As a general rule, if you are a UK resident taxpayer and under the age of 75, you can contribute as much as you earn each year to your pensions, up to the annual allowance set by the government at that time.

If you look at the ISA and the pension alongside each other over 25 years you can see therefore that the pension, because of the basic rate tax relief received, has a huge advantage as, put quite simply, more is going into the pot each and every month.

Over 25 years this makes the following difference, if we compare the figures from the last chapter to the pension figures:

Investment return	ISA fund value	Pension fund value
2.5% per year	£139,835	£174,793
4.0% per year	£172,748	£215,935
5.5% per year	£215,725	£269,656
7.0% per year	£272,184	£340,230

Note: This comparison is for illustration only and makes a lot of basic assumptions. For example, it assumes you would use exactly the same investment approach, all the charges and costs of the ISA and pension are the same and that you can make such contributions – and of course nothing changes in legislation over 25 years and so on. However, the comparison shows the impact of the tax relief on how much is accumulated – all other things being equal – in the different structures. You might note the comparative pension figure is always at least 20% higher. That's because the value of the tax relief amounts to 20% more going into the pension.

Taking the 5.5% per year growth figure, for exactly the same pay out each and every month, your pot is about £54,000 bigger.

The 'problem' is that, with the pension, if you then withdraw the whole sum (assuming you are age 55 or over) when you get to the end of 25 years and want to pay off your mortgage, you can only take 25% of the sum tax free but the rest is taxed at your highest marginal rate of income tax.

Assume your pension fund was worth £300,000. You could withdraw £75,000 tax free. The rest – £225,000 – is added to your income that year and you could easily lose the best part of £100,000 of this in taxation. This is a highly alarming prospect and one again where I would always recommend that an individual take professional financial planning advice before actually going down the road of taking substantial withdrawals from a pension fund to ensure that withdrawals are drawn down as tax efficiently and as responsibly as possible.

Your alternative could be to take the £75,000 tax free straight away, use this amount to pay down your mortgage by this amount and then stagger taking the taxable pension withdrawals slowly over time, possibly (and hopefully) at a lower tax rate, thereby reducing the pain of the taxation burden. However, this does assume you have the mortgage flexibility to do so.

It is quite clear therefore that the pension option has a huge advantage with the contribution boost but this is decimated if it is lost at the point of withdrawal by excessive taxation. In fact it could be worse than losing the advantage – it could turn into an overall disadvantage.

Where does this leave us? In a way this takes us straight back to a central theme of this book: there are no right or wrong ways of approaching either the payment or structure of a mortgage or – where desired – the way to accelerate a mortgage repayment.

What this does, hopefully, is show that pensions could have a place as a savings vehicle for their inherent tax advantages outlined above.

The 'smart' thing to do is to work out, wherever possible, how to maximise and use the distinctive advantages of either the pension or the ISA – or both together – to work best in your situation.

For example, imagine you are the person described earlier, paying a £200,000 mortgage started in 2005, due to be paid in 2030, and you are using an interest only loan plus an ISA savings vehicle to manage your position. You are paying £336 into the ISA every month.

Suddenly, perhaps due to an inheritance or the sale of a business, you have significant extra sums to put towards the monthly payments, let's say £1,800 per month, but you are also very light on pension provision, having invested little over the years towards your retirement. You are 50 years of age.

Now in this instance you might view it wise to start thinking seriously about retirement and adding a pension alongside the mortgage arrangement. You decide to place the excess amount, the additional sum of £1,800 per month, into a pension, because this will be 'grossed up' by the addition of basic rate tax relief to £2,250 per month. You pay this for seven years or to a point where your pension fund becomes worth, say, £200,000. Now you stop paying into the pension, cash in your ISAs, take 25% from your pension tax free, combine the two and pay off, or partially pay off, your mortgage.

This is a very simplistic view of using a pension as long-term financial plans will mean that the mortgage is just a small part of your overall objectives but let's look again at the basic objective here – of clearing the mortgage as quickly as possible.

You have taken 25% from your pension fund – albeit tax free – to do this. But you still have £150,000 left in the pension and now also have a pension pot to draw upon as and when you need to in the future.

That's how you might use a pension dynamically in the context of repaying a mortgage.

Before we move on any further let's also consider some of the other attractions and benefits of investing in a pension contract.

The tax relief I have discussed earlier in this chapter is the **basic rate of tax** applied on the pension contribution made. If you are a higher earner and therefore pay a higher level of income tax because of these higher earnings, you are currently able to claim a higher level of tax relief on any pension contributions.

Bear in mind that all this detail could change in future UK budgets. At the time of writing, subject to contribution limits you are able to receive tax relief on pension contributions at the highest rate of income tax paid, maybe as much as 45% of the gross pension contribution.

The way the tax relief is calculated is that you receive the basic rate tax relief added to your initial contribution and you are then potentially entitled to claim additional tax relief via your self-assessment tax return if you are paying higher levels of tax.

I have ignored this point throughout the earlier parts of this chapter, but it has to be noted that if you do qualify as a higher earner and therefore can claim additional tax reliefs, the arguments in favour of using pensions increase dramatically. The added value increases and the like-for-like difference illustrated earlier with ISAs swings dramatically in favour of investing in pensions.

Pensions have a very valuable place in many mortgage repayment scenarios. This is mainly due to the need to build up a retirement pot which can later be used to maintain income in retirement, but also because of the generous tax-free cash allowance that can be taken and of course the potentially highly generous tax-relief benefits that can be received when making pension contributions themselves.

Chapter 18 - Combined efforts – mix 'n' match

Possibly the most important message I hope you will take away from reading these pages is what we have covered in the last two chapters: that every situation needs to be assessed on its own merits and that it is very likely any plan to pay your mortgage off early will involve combining a variety of methods in the overall repayment plan.

This chapter is about the latter – the fact that it normally makes sense to mix and match the products, savings vehicles and overpayment facilities you use to meet your goals.

The wish to clear a mortgage as quickly as possible is unlikely to be your only financial or lifestyle goal. Assuming this is the case and you have multiple goals, then your plans will have to cater for all these, to respect your priorities and to carefully balance the individual goals against one another.

The best example of this is most likely to be the other 'big goal' you will have, which is to retire comfortably. Defining what that means will be a personal matter, but for many this could include retiring early or at a point of your choosing.

To achieve both an early mortgage repayment and an early retirement clearly involves achieving a decent level of wealth and the repayment of any outstanding debt. This could come from a combination of long-term regular savings as well as good financial discipline, including investing your savings as efficiently as possible, maximising pay-outs from a business shareholding, releasing a valuable company pension, the receipt of an inheritance, selling rental property or some other windfall created by your efforts.

In turn this makes it likely that you will use different financial products, including ISAs and pensions, insurance policies and other types of investment funds.

How you mix the use of these products over time will be dictated by your goals, your attitude to risk, your tax position and your wider family situation.

So when it comes to the objective of accelerating the repayment of a mortgage this will be one goal among many. The reality is that what you are aiming to do is create wealth within your overall framework at a targeted date or stage when you **can** pay off your mortgage early.

With nearly all goals – and within financial planning as a whole – having flexibility and options is an important factor – as is having your eggs in more than one basket. This suggests that using different savings and investment products and vehicles working alongside each other is a sensible approach.

I would recommend that, in the context of striving to clear a mortgage, you aim to use this approach as your starting point. Look to work to an overall plan which combines the advantages of different savings products, their flexibilities and tax advantages into an optimum approach that works best for your situation.

As an example, if you are using a capital repayment mortgage as the method to pay your mortgage down over its agreed term, you want to look at reducing this term (i.e. to clear the mortgage early) and you are not maximising your pension contributions, then you should explore the pension option described earlier, as this may have considerably greater advantages than merely upping the capital repayment monthly amount.

To summarise I would suggest that a mix and match approach has its merits. It should be viable for most people and you should probably explore the different options available to you for the following reasons:

- It avoids having all your eggs in one basket.
- It helps reduce risk.
- It allows you to optimise your tax position.
- It is likely to offer greater flexibility, especially if things change in the future.
- It respects the fact that your financial planning is likely to represent plans to meet all your goals, not just those for your mortgage.

Remember, take professional financial planning advice to ensure that you choose wisely and make the correct decisions for your own circumstances.

Chapter 19 - Protecting your mortgage

One of the biggest financial mistakes anyone can make is to assume that things won't change. As I have already intimated and totally concur with is that 'the only constant in life is change'.

It is easy to look back and see what has happened in the past. Indeed it is easy to look at one's financial situation today and know how you got to where you are now **but it is very difficult, if not impossible, to predict what is going to happen in the future.** This applies whether you are considering investment returns, market movements, inflation and interest rates or house prices – **or, crucially, your own circumstances.**

If you have a mortgage you simply have to ask (and answer) the question, what if? Let's apply this to a series of possible risks:

- **What would happen if you or your partner were to lose their job?** According to Linkedin, the average worker currently will have held ten different jobs before the age of forty so the likelihood of some employment changes during a 25-year mortgage term is quite likely. Now voluntary changes in employment are fine as you can plan for short-term fluctuations in income but a period of unexpected unemployment, in the form of redundancy for example, can have dramatic short-term ramifications for the health of your finances.

- **What if you fall off a ladder and seriously injure yourself or have a sustained period of sickness?** This may seem like a silly question but life has a tendency to throw us a curve ball from time to time. Again, the 'what if?' question needs to be considered when thinking about signing yourself up to a long-term financial commitment such as a mortgage. Many if not most employers provide relatively limited in-house sickness benefits these days and most people would have to rely solely on statutory sick pay should they be too ill to work. At the time of writing this book statutory sick pay is a maximum of £92.05 per week and is paid for a maximum of 28 weeks. In order to qualify for SSP you need to have been off work for four days or more in a row (excluding non-working days – weekends etc.). Seeing your income drop dramatically in a very short period of time could potentially be disastrous for your finances if you do not have some level of savings behind you as a safety net or have a family member that can help you get over a period of long-term sickness and the associated loss of income that this could result in. Remember that mortgage lenders have little patience for people's problems – their greatest priority is to get their money each month!

- **What if you become unable to make financial decisions because of poor mental health?** Disability doesn't just show itself in physical form. According to www.mentalhealth.org.uk depression is the predominant mental health problem worldwide followed by anxiety, schizophrenia and bipolar disorder. In 2013 depression was the second leading cause of years lived with a disability worldwide, behind lower back pain. As discussed previously, a mortgage commitment is indeed a commitment for a period of many years. None of us know what is around the corner and what problems we or our families will be faced with from one year to the next and how those problems may impact on our day-to-day finances.

- **What if you or your spouse dies unexpectedly?** This undoubtedly is the most extreme scenario but one I have seen over the years. I can recall a situation where a husband who was the sole earner in the house passed away suddenly through illness. His wife and two children were suddenly faced with a situation where not only had they lost their husband and father but they had lost their financial stability at the same time. Children still need to be fed, the bills keep coming and the mortgage will still need to be paid at a time when a parent has been lost and the monthly salary is no longer coming in.

When I started arranging mortgages over 25 years ago mortgage lenders often only offered mortgages with a life assurance assigned to them as part of the mortgage deal, so that *they* knew the mortgage would be cleared if a borrower died.

However, this was deemed to be too expensive to administer by lenders and over the years this practice was phased out. It is now up to individual borrowers to make their own arrangements.

Whatever stage you are at in your mortgage 'journey' you have to look hard at the consequences of something unexpected happening where you or your loved ones are left unable to pay the mortgage.

This means considering having life assurance cover, serious illness insurance, income protection insurance, possibly redundancy cover (if available) and in many cases a power of attorney.

I am not going to go through an extensive list of what you should and shouldn't have in this book to cover these various scenarios but I would always recommend that you take professional advice from a suitably qualified financial adviser who will ensure that your individual circumstances are taken into consideration and that you are adequately covered.

The power of attorney is an interesting recommendation because it is not an area that many people consider. However, in an age where dementia is, sadly, so prevalent having a solution in place should this happen to you or a family member is financially prudent and eminently sensible.

The power of attorney is a document which states who you appoint to take control of your finances should something happen to you in this way, in other words should you lose your ability to manage your finances and make day-to-day financial decisions.

Of course, this also leads onto the final point with regard to protecting your mortgage – make sure you have a will. If you or your partner pass away matters can get very complicated and a mortgage is one of those many complicating factors.

Again if in doubt seek professional advice.

Chapter 20 - One size does not fit all – do what is right for you!

The idea of paying off your mortgage early is a wonderful goal to work towards. It can be started at any stage, even the very earliest stages soon after you start off down the mortgage road.

Once the goal is set then the ways you go about reaching it will be entirely dependent on your own circumstances.

As alluded to throughout this book, there are many factors to take into account and many options to consider to reach your objective. No two sets of circumstances will be exactly the same and even small differences can lead to different methods being pursued.

It is important to set your mortgage targets in relation to your wider financial and lifestyle goals. The word 'lifestyle' is relevant because ultimately your money and finances have to be representative of what you want out of your life. This correlation between your life and finances is crucial.

The line between goals and plans works something like this: lifestyle goals – financial goals – your existing financial position – all lead to your planning decisions.

Subtle shifts along this line can bring about significant changes in your planning and alter exactly what you do. This is why two people in broadly similar situations with regard to their mortgages, both wanting to pay off their mortgage early, would employ different strategies to do so.

This occurs because something within their wider circumstances or lifestyle goals is different and that difference (which could be subtle) changes the planning decisions and methods.

It is also important to note that nothing is static. Just as the planning decisions and actions will change from person to person for the reasons outlined above, so actions and decisions may change within a person's own lifetime.

It is perfectly possible to start off with a strategy of paying off a mortgage using a capital repayment basis, then introduce a pension into the equation later down the line to accelerate the clearance of the mortgage, then revert to a capital repayment basis again later. There are reasons why this could happen and why the strategy may change over the years.

Remember, there is also no right way or wrong way of doing something.

With an interest only mortgage backed by a repayment using a savings vehicle (e.g. an ISA), a great deal of dependence will be on the investment return and performance of the ISA. Assuming some form of investment risk is taken (to try and generate higher returns) the performance of the ISA, the annual growth, will be unknown in advance.

It will only be with the benefit of time and hindsight that things will become known. Once known it is easy to answer whether using the ISA was a better option than a capital repayment mortgage. Likewise after time you will know whether you would have been better off using a fixed rate of interest or a variable rate.

None of these are known in advance, so you cannot have certainty that any chosen pathway or structure you use is better than any other when you make your decisions.

This lack of a right or wrong way of doing things needs to be respected. Your aim is to work out what is best for you given your current circumstances, your future goals – both lifestyle and financial – and your best estimate of what is likely to happen.

On this last point, you should be careful to make sure those assumptions are risk-adjusted ones – do not do anything based on a headstrong belief. For example, do not assume interest rates will remain at their current levels or will always be low. Or that property prices cannot fall.

Your planning should have great respect for possible significant changes in circumstances, both your own and those of the wider world around you.

The key to all this is to work very closely on your own financial plan, making sure it is completely tailored to your overall position, requirements and objectives. In this respect, your financial planning should be unique.

Conclusion

Aiming to clear your mortgage as early as possible is a fine ambition to introduce into your thinking. But it may not always be viable or even, in some cases, desirable.

Other financial planning considerations and other goals need to be taken into account. Assuming, though, that you have this ambition and the means to achieve it, then you will want to formulate a plan to make it happen. That plan will be unique to your circumstances. It could easily incorporate the use of different financial products at different stages.

There will be much to weigh up and using expert advice to help you could make all the difference.

The financial impact of paying off a mortgage early can transform an individual's situation, especially in the context of retirement income and plans.

It can also prove hugely satisfying from a non-financial point of view. For many people the whole idea of having unfettered and outright ownership of their own home is a hugely desirable outcome simply based on the psychological merits.

I hope that some of the ideas, thoughts, suggestions and information provided throughout this book have contributed to your understanding of this subject and have helped to plant ideas in your mind as to how you should go about it.

I wish you all the very best in your endeavours.

Darren Fisher
Author

Sources for Mortgage Calculations:

- *Money Saving Expert*
- *Barclays Bank Offset Calculator*

Printed in Great Britain
by Amazon

14161400R00075